GREAT BRITISH FOOD REVIVAL

MICHEL ROUX JR. ❧ MARY BERRY

RAYMOND BLANC ❧ GREGG WALLACE

YOTAM OTTOLENGHI ❧ ANTONIO CARLUCCIO

VALENTINE WARNER ❧ AINSLEY HARRIOTT

JOHN TORODE ❧ CLARISSA DICKSON WRIGHT

ANGELA HARTNETT ❧ RICHARD CORRIGAN

MATT TEBBUTT ❧ JAMES MARTIN

GARY RHODES ❧ JASON ATHERTON

with

BLANCHE VAUGHAN

First published in hardback in Great Britain in 2011 by
Weidenfeld & Nicolson, an imprint of the Orion Publishing Group Lt
Orion House, 5 Upper St Martin's Lane, London WC2H 9EA
an Hachette UK Company

1 3 5 7 9 10 8 6 4 2

A CIP catalogue record for this book is available from the British Library.

Photography by Andrew Hayes-Watkins
Design & Art Direction by Kate Barr
Art Editor Natasha Webber
Editorial by Amanda Harris, Sally Coleman, Nicola Crossley, Ione Walder and Cherry Ekins

978 0 297 86764 7

Printed and bound in Germany

The Orion Publishing Group's policy is to use papers that are natural, renewable and recyclable and made from wood grown in sustainable forests. The logging and manufacturing processes are expected to conform to environmental regulations of the country of origin.

www.orionbooks.co.uk

CONTENTS

INTRODUCTION

Our nation produces the best ingredients in the world. This inspiring book is a celebration of Britain's heritage varieties and native breeds that deserve to be cooked with pleasure and eaten with great relish.

Britain's larder has so much to offer, more flavour and taste than any cheap imports, and 16 of the best chefs in the country have joined forces to champion our amazing home-grown food. They have written recipes that make the most of our fabulous British ingredients.

In this cookbook Michel Roux Jr. returns to where he grew up in Kent to celebrate pears; Mary Berry shows us how indispensable fresh herbs are in both sweet and savoury dishes; Raymond Blanc picks plums to dry and marinate with pork and to preserve for the winter in spicy chutneys; Gregg Wallace reminds us of the pleasures of beautiful rhubarb, showing us how many savoury dishes we can make before we even begin to think of sweet; Yotam Ottolenghi gives a Middle Eastern twist to the walnut and covers the cobnut in creamy, crumble glory; Antonio Carluccio surprises us with the versatility of beetroot in soufflés and puddings; Valentine Warner picks cockles and mussels fresh from our shores and gives us his luxurious and warming version of moules marinière; Ainsley Harriott pods fresh peas to make vibrant salads and colourful mash-up; John Torode champions beef to ensure our native rare breeds are pulled back from the brink of extinction; Angela Hartnett works her magic on turkey, showing us how to use it beyond Christmas; Richard Corrigan speaks out for the wonderful flavour of mackerel and shows us how to home-smoke our own; Matt Tebbutt finds fabulous ways with currants, teaming this jewel-like fruit with wild duck and with a home-made whisky cordial; James Martin takes us beyond hens' eggs to share the taste of cooking with duck and quail eggs; Gary Rhodes teaches us how to cook his famous cherry clafoutis and finally, Jason Atherton gives us many reasons to love the sophisticated versatility of cabbage.

Now it's up to us to choose these wonderful ingredients, to grow or buy them and to cook with them. Be inspired by the recipes from these celebrated chefs. Get creative in the kitchen and enjoy our nation's abundant resources.

PEARS

with RECIPES *by* MICHEL ROUX JR.

The pear is a wonderful and versatile fruit. There are pears for cooking and pears for eating raw, and they can be used in a huge variety of dishes. They are wonderful in salads, where their sweetness contrasts with bitter leaves and salty blue cheese such as Roquefort or Stilton. Italians eat thin slices of pear with pecorino cheese and honey. Pears also taste fantastic with rich meat such as beef, duck or game. In winter, they can be made into cheering, colourful puddings; pears poached in red wine or cooked with sweet Marsala and served with rich cream or baked in tarts with almonds or walnuts. They can even be used for drinks such as pear brandy, pear liqueur or the bubbly pear and Prosecco cocktail on page 18.

The Victorians enjoyed over 600 varieties of pear; now the supermarket shelves limit us to a handful of varieties and, of those, very few will be British. The sad truth of pears today is that 90% of the UK's orchards have been pulled up for development or for other types of agriculture and now 80% of the pears we buy are imported.

However, dedicated British producers are working hard to make the British pear available for more months of the year and to bring back a selection of heritage varieties. The Conference pear will always be popular for its grainy texture, juiciness and versatility in being good for cooking and eating raw. But another pear to look out for is the Black Worcester, with a mahogany skin and russet freckles. Puréed or baked, it is a perfect cooking pear. Or perhaps, intrigued by the names, you might enjoy the different flavours and textures of Winter Nellis and Louis Bonne of Jersey.

Other pears that need our support are Perry, or 'Hartpury' pears, which hail from the three counties of Worcestershire, Herefordshire and Gloucestershire. These are the pear varieties used to make Perry and Perry cider. But the commercially produced pear cider we drink today isn't even made with Perry pears; eating pears are used instead because they are sweeter. So to preserve the remaining Perry orchards we need to look out for drinks made with the Perry pear.

Whether it's eating fresh, cooking with pears or enjoying a glass of Perry, it's time to support these dedicated pear farmers who are resurrecting our heritage varieties. When you have the option to buy British, do so, and try eating different varieties to discover the special characteristics of each one. A British pear in season will always be more enjoyable than an imported pear at the wrong time of year.

PEAR TART
with STILTON *and* PISTACHIOS

Pears are a well-known accompaniment to cheese but this recipe takes it to another level. Cooking pears in red wine and spices is a classic dessert that I love and only surpassed by serving them as a sophisticated, classy starter that is actually very easy to achieve.

Perfect with blue cheese of your choice but equally as good with mature hard cheese such as pecorino, Cantal or even Cheddar. Most good delis will stock pistachio oil but if you can't get your hands on some, then a drizzle of strong extra virgin olive oil will work a treat. Choose a slightly firm Williams or Cornice for this recipe and for a really deep red wine colour, cook the pears a couple of days in advance and keep in the fridge until needed. *Michel Roux Jr.*

Serves 4		
	120g puff pastry, plus flour for dusting	150g Stilton cheese, crumbled
	2 pears, peeled	60g pistachios, shelled and chopped
	500ml red wine	baby salad leaves
	80g caster sugar	olive oil
	2 tbsp blackcurrant liqueur	lemon juice
	1 cinnamon stick	salt and pepper
	1 clove	pistachio oil
	1 dried red chilli	

Preheat the oven to 180°C/350°F/Gas 4. Roll out the puff pastry on a lightly floured surface to 2mm thick and then prick all over with a fork. Place the pastry in between two non-stick baking sheets and cook in the oven until golden and crisp. Leave to cool and then cut into four rectangles.

Put the pears in a saucepan with the wine, sugar, liqueur, spices and chilli. Quickly bring to the boil and then cover with greaseproof paper and simmer until tender, turning over the pears several times during cooking. Remove from the heat and leave to cool.

Once cool, drain and reserve the cooking liquid. Cut the pears in half and core them, cut into slices and place on the rectangles of puff pastry.

Return the saucepan to the heat and quickly boil the cooking liquid until syrupy.

Sprinkle the Stilton and pistachios over the pear. Garnish with a few salad leaves seasoned with olive oil, lemon juice, salt and pepper. Serve with a drizzle of the syrupy red wine sauce and pistachio oil.

BRAISED BEEF CHEEKS
with PEAR *and* BITTER CHOCOLATE SAUCE

At a first glance this may sound like an odd combination but I guarantee that once you have tasted this you will, like me, be in food heaven! The beef cheeks can be ordered from your local butcher and when slow cooked are the most tender and succulent of cuts. The sauce is rich and sweet from the port and chocolate but brought together in perfect unison by the slightly crunchy, sharp pears. *Michel Roux Jr.*

Serves 4

Bean purée
80g dry white beans
2 bay leaves
sprig of rosemary
salt
small knob of butter
200ml double cream, heated to a boil

2 pears
butter, for frying
2 beef cheeks, trimmed and cut into
   four equal-sized pieces

salt
oil, for frying
1 onion, sliced
1 garlic clove, sliced
1 glass of port
juice of 1 orange, and a little zest
2 litres beef stock
1 tbsp cracked black pepper
16 button onions, peeled
butter, for cooking
60g extra bitter chocolate 70% cocoa,
   broken into squares

Soak the beans overnight and then drain. Place the beans in a pan of fresh water and bring to the boil. Add the bay leaves and rosemary, cover with greaseproof paper and simmer until cooked.

Remove the herbs and drain the beans over a bowl to reserve the cooking liquid, then put the beans in a blender. Season with salt and blitz with a little butter and cream until silky smooth, adding some of the cooking liquid if necessary.

Peel and core the pears, cut into 1.5cm cubes and cover with a little lemon juice and water until needed. The pear peel can be mixed in with the beef while it is cooking in the oven.

Preheat the oven to 180°C/350°F/Gas 4. Season the beef cheeks with salt and fry in a little oil until coloured on all sides. Remove the meat and, in the same pan, fry the onion and garlic until brown. Return the meat to the pan and at the same time deglaze the pan with the port and orange juice. Cook until syrupy and then add the stock, pepper and orange zest. Cover with greaseproof paper and place in the oven for 3 hours or until tender.

When the beef is nearly ready, cook the button onions in a little seasoned water and butter, and in another pan fry the pear cubes in a little butter.

When the beef is cooked, remove from the pan, place a fine sieve over a bowl and strain the cooking liquid. Pour the liquid into a pan, bring to a boil and reduce the sauce to a syrupy consistency. Then whisk in the chocolate and a couple of knobs of butter. Dress the plate with a spoonful of white bean purée, the cooked pear cubes and the button onions. Lay a piece of beef cheek on each plate and spoon round the rich, dark sauce.

PEAR OMELETTE SOUFFLÉ
with SALTED BUTTER CARAMEL SAUCE

There is something special about soufflés and this one is no exception, it is quite simply delicious. This recipe is so easy that everyone can impress their friends with light, fluffy flavourful soufflés every time. The choice of pears does not really matter but they should be a little firm and the addition of a pear brandy really does finish off the dish beautifully. *Michel Roux Jr.*

Serves 4		
	360g caster sugar	8 free range egg whites
	500ml water	butter, for greasing
	1 vanilla pod, split in half	
	juice of 1 lemon	*Caramel sauce*
	6 pears, peeled, cored and halved	75g salted butter
	4 tbsp pear brandy	100g unrefined caster sugar
	2 tbsp cornflour	400ml double cream

You will need four small (10–12cm) omelette pans with ovenproof handles.

Preheat the oven to 190°C/375°F/Gas 5. In a pan, place 4 tablespoons of caster sugar, the water and split vanilla pod and boil for 5 minutes. Add the lemon juice and pears to the pan and simmer until tender. Remove from the heat and allow to cool. Remove the pears and reserve the poaching syrup.

Once cooled, cut off the thickest part of each pear and thinly slice. Pour the pear brandy into a dish and put the pear slices into the brandy to steep. Take the remaining parts of the pears, place in a blender and blitz until smooth. Transfer the purée to a pan, bring to the boil and thicken with the cornflour moistened with a little of the poaching syrup.

For the sauce, melt the butter and sugar in a pan until rich golden brown in colour and caramel scented. Pour on the cream and bring to a boil. Take off the heat, pass through a fine sieve and keep warm.

Whisk up the egg whites and add the rest of the sugar a spoonful at a time. Continue to whisk until stiff and smooth. Fold the whisked whites in to the pear purée, making sure not to overwork it. Divide the mixture into the four small, hot, buttered omelette pans. Leave on the hob on a low heat for a few seconds then put in the oven for 6 minutes until cooked.

When you are nearly ready to serve, put the pear slices and brandy in a small saucepan and warm gently on a low heat. Remove the pear slices with a slotted spoon and discard the brandy. Gently tip the omelette soufflés onto plates with the warmed pear slices and drizzle with the caramel sauce.

POACHED PEARS
in RED WINE

Serves 6

6 pears, peeled, cored and halved lengthways
500ml light red wine (Beaujolais works well)
4 tbsp sugar
1 cinnamon stick
4 cloves
1 vanilla pod, seeds scraped out
crème fraîche

Place the pears into a pan with a lid, large enough to hold them flat in one layer, and pour over the wine to cover. Add the sugar, cinnamon stick, cloves and vanilla seeds.

Bring to a gentle boil before turning down to a simmer and cover. Cook for 10–15 minutes, or until tender. (A good way to check this is by inserting a knife or skewer. If there is no resistance, the pear is ready.) Remove the pears from the liquor and set aside. Turn up the heat to a boil and cook to reduce the liquor to a light syrup.

Serve the pears with the syrup poured over the top and a dollop of crème fraîche.

PEAR TARTE TATIN

Serves 4   flour, for dusting
200g puff pastry
2–3 ripe pears
juice of ½ lemon
1 vanilla pod, seeds scraped out
100g caster sugar
50g unsalted butter, cut into small pieces

You will need a 25 x 4cm non-stick frying pan, with an ovenproof or detachable handle.

Preheat the oven to 200°C/400°F/Gas 6. On a lightly floured surface, roll the pastry into a circle 5mm thick and large enough to cover the top of the pan with a little extra to hang over the side. Set the rolled pastry aside to rest.

Peel and core the pears and slice into eighths. Sprinkle with lemon juice to prevent them from discolouring. Scatter the vanilla seeds over the pear slices.

In the frying pan, melt the sugar over a medium heat and when it starts to caramelise, add the pieces of butter one at a time. Continue cooking until all the butter has melted and you have a smooth, bubbling liquid.

Lay the pear slices in the frying pan, overlapping each other so that they cover the base of the pan. Continue cooking for 2 minutes to brown the bottom of the pears in the caramel but do not to let them burn.

Remove the pan from the heat and lay the pastry over the top of the pears. Tuck any excess pastry around the pears and into the pan. Place the pan on a baking sheet and bake for 20–25 minutes or until the pastry is golden and crisp.

To serve, place a plate that fits snugly over the top of the pan. Hold the pan and plate firmly together and quickly flip the pan upside down on top of the plate. Carefully lift away the pan, leaving the tart pear-side up on the plate. Delicious with vanilla ice cream.

PEAR *and* PROSECCO COCKTAIL

Serves 6–8   3 very ripe pears, peeled, cored and cut into large chunks
juice of ½ lemon
3–4 tsp sugar
1 bottle of Prosecco, chilled

Put the pear chunks in a bowl and squeeze over a little lemon juice and sprinkle on some of the sugar. Using a hand blender, blitz to a purée.

Sieve the purée into a bowl and taste. Depending on the sweetness of the pears you may need to add either a little more lemon or sugar.

To serve, put 2 tablespoons of the pear purée into the bottom of a high-ball glass and pour over the chilled Prosecco to about halfway up the glass.

HERBS
with RECIPES *by* MARY BERRY

Why do we reach for the dried herbs when they're incomparable to fresh? We need to be more experimental; give fresh a go and banish tasteless dried imposters.

In pre-Christian Britain, the Druids used herbs to make rudimentary medicines. By the Middle Ages, they were commonly used for casting spells and even as love potions. Rosemary was carried by Elizabethan sweethearts as a sign of fidelity and bouquets of it were dipped in gold as presents for wedding guests.

But where herbs really need celebrating is in cooking. They are wonderful flavour-enhancers and give colour and zest to a dish. They make fabulous sauces; try a vibrant green herb sauce, punchy with cornichons and vinegar or a tangy sorrel and spinach sauce as an accompaniment to fish. Highly fragrant herbs like thyme or rosemary are excellent with rich, creamy tastes like goat's cheese or use them with apples, baked in a roasting tray with pork. For puddings, an ice cream infused with lemon balm is a perfect balance of sweetness and tang.

Herbs are available to gather for free in our own countryside; using a good book as a guide, there are all sorts of things you can find. Wild sorrel, mint, marjoram, thyme and rosemary are just a few.

Lemon balm grows all year round and its textured lemon-scented leaves can be picked fresh before the plant flowers and used fresh or dried. The leaves can used in sweet or savoury dishes or infused in hot water to make a refreshing tea.

Herbs that are difficult to get hold of, you can grow yourself, even with the tiniest amount of space. The important thing to remember is to think seasonally, then you will always be eating herbs that are fresh and at their best. Enjoy using hardier herbs like bay, fennel, parsley, rosemary, thyme and winter savory in the colder months. Then, when spring and summer bring new growth of plants like basil, dill, marjoram, mint and sorrel, you will have a whole range of different flavours to enjoy cooking with. Be creative and use herbs in different ways to make the best of what is available for each season of the year.

GOAT'S CHEESE, PEPPERS *and* THYME GALETTES *with* ONION MARMALADE

I make a couple of these galettes for a quick lunch for six and serve with a dressed mixed-leaf salad. Use just the leaves from the thyme – I prefer broad-leaved thyme because it has an excellent flavour and is easy to pick off the stalk. If using bought thyme, it will have been grown quickly and therefore the stalks will be young and tender so just finely chop both the leaves and stalks and it will have a less piquant flavour. If time is short, use onion marmalade from a jar and bottled peppers in oil. *Mary Berry*

Serves 6

Onion marmalade
2 tbsp olive oil
3 large onions, sliced
1 tbsp sugar
1 tbsp balsamic vinegar
salt and pepper

Galettes
3 red peppers
olive oil
500g block of ready-made all-butter puff pastry (use two-thirds and freeze the remaining third for another day)
2 x 150g tubs soft goat's cheese
2 tbsp fresh broad-leaf thyme
1 egg, beaten

Preheat the oven to 200°C/400°F/Gas 6 and put a heavy baking sheet in the oven to get hot.

To make the onion marmalade, heat the oil in a non-stick frying pan over a high heat. Add the onion and fry for a few minutes. Sprinkle in the sugar, vinegar and season with salt and pepper. Cover and lower the heat for about 20 minutes or until soft. If liquid has come out, remove the lid and evaporate. Set aside to cool.

Cut each pepper in half, remove the stalk and seeds and lay, cut-side down on a baking sheet. Drizzle with a little olive oil and roast in the preheated oven for about 30 minutes or until the skins are black. Transfer to a plastic bag and seal. Once cold, peel away the skin and slice into thin strips.

Roll the pastry thinly on a non-stick sheet of paper to a square about 30 x 30cm. Cut the pastry in half and carefully lift the pastry squares and paper onto the hot baking sheet. Prick the squares with a fork leaving a 2cm border around the edges. Spread the goat's cheese within each border and sprinkle over the thyme leaves. Spoon over the onion marmalade and scatter with pepper strips. Brush the outside borders with beaten egg.

Bake in the oven for about 20–25 minutes until the pastry is crispy.

Serve warm with a dressed mixed leaf salad.

SALMON FILLET
with FRESH SORREL *and* SPINACH SAUCE

Sorrell has a sharp crisp taste and is delicious when combined with spinach. Sometimes I add a dash of sugar which balances the sauce. I like to use buckler-leaf or French sorrel. The more usual sorrel has a pointed leaf; both should have the flowery stems cut off when they appear as this encourages further growth. Buckler-leaf sorrel is a low-growing species with shield-shaped, decorative leaves perfect for scattering in green leaf salads. This sauce goes well with salmon trout, salmon and sea bass. The flour is added to the sauce to prevent it from splitting. The sauce can be made a day ahead without adding the spinach and sorrel. Next day, reheat and add the spinach and sorrel, if added too soon the lovely bright green with turn grey! *Mary Berry*

Serves 6

6 salmon fillets
butter
6 slices of lemon

Sauce
75g butter, melted
juice of ½ lemon

2 tsp plain flour
300ml half-fat crème fraîche
1 free range egg yolk
salt and black pepper
25g sorrel, finely chopped
25g spinach, finely chopped

Preheat the oven to 180°C/350°F/Gas 4. Place each salmon fillet on top of a piece of parchment paper, place a knob of butter and slice of lemon on top of the fish. Make a parcel from the parchment paper, leaving enough room for the steam to circulate during cooking, and then fold over the edges of the paper to seal. Cook in the oven for 20 minutes.

Put the melted butter, juice, flour, crème fraîche and egg yolk into a food processor or blender and whiz until smooth. Season with salt and pepper and whiz again.

Pour the blended mixture into a heatproof bowl and sit the bowl over a pan of barely simmering water. Whisk continuously over a low heat for about 10 minutes until thick and fluffy. Add the sorrel and spinach and heat gently for a few minutes. Check the seasoning and serve hot with the cooked salmon.

LEMON MERINGUE ICE CREAM
with LEMON BALM

A good way to turn broken meringues into a stunning dessert. Lemon balm is a lemon-scented member of the mint family and comes in two varieties – plain green and variegated. It grows vigorously so should not be allowed to flower and should be cut down once during the season. New growth will appear in two or three weeks and the young leaves are best to use in recipes. *Mary Berry*

Serves 6 | 50g meringues, they can be broken ones
300ml double cream
zest and juice of 1 lemon
1 jar of home-made or luxury lemon curd
2 tbsp chopped fresh lemon balm
3 passion fruit, halved, pulp and seeds scooped out
sprigs of lemon balm, to garnish

You will need a 450g loaf tin lined with clingfilm overlapping the sides.

Lightly break up the meringues into chunky pieces. Whisk the cream lightly until the whisk leaves a trail, add the zest, juice and half a jar of lemon curd to the cream and finally gently fold in the meringue and lemon balm.

Spoon the lemon meringue mixture into the loaf tin, cover with clingfilm and then freeze for at least 6 hours.

If the ice cream has been in the freezer overnight or longer, bring to room temperature for about 10–15 minutes before turning out onto a plate. Lift the ice cream from the loaf tin, invert it onto a board and remove the clingfilm. Dip a sharp knife in boiling water and slice the loaf into fairly thick slices. Cut each slice on the diagonal to give two triangles.

Mix the other half of the jar of lemon curd with the pulp and seeds from the passion fruit.

Place two triangles of ice cream on a plate and top with a spoonful of the mixed lemon curd and passion fruit. Decorate with sprigs of lemon balm. This is wonderful served with a raspberry coulis or summer berries.

GREEN HERB SAUCE

A wonderful sauce to go with roasted or cold meats.

Serves 4–6
1 large bunch of parsley, leaves picked from the stem
1 small bunch of marjoram, leaves picked from the stem
½ small bunch of mint, leaves picked from the stem
½ small bunch of dill
¼ small bunch of tarragon, leaves picked from the stem
200ml or more olive oil
2 tsp capers, chopped
4 anchovy fillets, chopped
3–4 cornichons, chopped
1 garlic clove, crushed to a paste with salt
black pepper

Chop all the herbs together by hand, to make a fine, green mixture. Put the chopped herbs into a bowl and add the olive oil. Stir well to coat, to prevent their discolouring.

Stir in the capers, anchovies, cornichons and garlic paste. Pour over some more oil to make a loose mixture and season with a little pepper.

PARSLEY *and* FENNEL SEED SAUCE

A delicious sauce to serve with pork.

Serves 4–6
1 bunch of parsley, finely chopped
2 tsp fennel seeds, ground to a powder
1 garlic clove, crushed to a paste with salt
5 tbsp olive oil
juice of ½ lemon
sea salt and black pepper

In a bowl, or a pestle and mortar, crush the chopped parsley, fennel seed powder and garlic together and make a loose sauce by adding the oil and lemon juice. Season well with salt and pepper.

PLUMS
with RECIPES *by* RAYMOND BLANC

Sweet plums picked ripe from the tree; juicy greengages; little purple damsons; tart, black wild sloes; these little fruit are an integral part of the British countryside. Each variety has a beautiful colour palette which ranges from green to golden-yellow, from pink to blue-purple and delicious flavours from tart to floral and sweet.

Plums can be poached, baked in a tart and eaten with cream, or made into delicate rippled ice cream. Plums become less sweet when they're cooked, so give a wonderful balance to rich meat dishes like roast pork. They are also perfect preserving fruit, either made into sharp chutneys or pickles to serve with cold meats or pâtés or preserved as thick, sweet jams.

Plums were grown in the orchards of medieval monasteries and the Victorian love affair with the plum lives on in the enduring variety 'Victoria'. However, in the last 25 years, the UK has lost 63% of its plum orchards. A far cry from 1920, when the Pershore Flower Show advertised itself as 'The Largest Plum Show on Earth'. Since then, the Vale of Evesham has lost 80% of its orchards and we are importing inferior plums from around the world.

To halt the decline, The Vale Landscape Heritage Trust has been set up to protect and preserve pockets of important and beautiful land and their aim is to rescue and rejuvenate some of these old orchards.

We can do our part by making the effort to enjoy these wonderful fruits in their season. The British plum tastes more succulent and sweet than anything imported and can be cooked and used in so many different ways. With a long history and heritage, the British plum deserves to be part of our summer fruit selection.

COUNTRY PÂTÉ
with SPICED PLUM CHUTNEY

Even France has discovered the chutney; built on the classic combination of sweet and acid flavours. It is easy to make and has the advantage of being able to be kept for up to one year (the sugar and vinegar are natural flavour enhancers and preservatives). This is one the best examples of the British love affair with the east. It goes with everything, from cold meats and cheese to pork pies and pâté. I am certainly a convert to chutneys. *Raymond Blanc*

Serves 12

Spiced plum chutney
35g root ginger, finely grated
1 white onion, chopped
1 star anise
2 cardamom pods, bruised with a knife
½ cinnamon stick
1 tsp salt
175g light brown muscovado sugar
200ml white wine vinegar
700g ripe plums, stoned and
   roughly chopped
700g Braeburn apples, peeled,
   cored and chopped

Pâté marinade
6g salt
2g black pepper, freshly ground
4 juniper berries, crushed
1g five-spice powder

½ tsp finely chopped thyme leaves
50ml white wine
2 tbsps Cognac brandy

Pâté meat
200g pork shoulder, boned and
   diced into 3cm pieces
200g pork belly, boned and
   diced into 3cm pieces
150g pork liver, cleaned and
   diced into 3cm pieces
100g chicken livers, cleaned and
   diced into 3cm pieces
150g pork back fat, diced into 3cm pieces
1 free range egg, beaten
20g pistachio nuts (or almonds/
   hazelnuts if you prefer)
1 bay leaf
2–3 sprigs of thyme

For the spiced plum chutney, you will need one 500ml sterilised glass jar with a vinegar-proof lid. For the pâté, you will need a terrine mould 23 x 9 x 8cm, greaseproof paper and a roasting tin to use as a bain-marie.

To make the chutney, put a large, heavy-based saucepan over a low heat. Put the ginger, onion, spices and salt into the pan and cook for about 8 minutes until the onions are semi-translucent. Increase to a medium heat, add the sugar and cook for a further 2 minutes to allow the sugar to melt. Add the vinegar and bring to the boil for 1 minute. Add the chopped fruit and bring back to the boil. Lower the heat and, uncovered, simmer gently for 1½–1¾ hours, stirring frequently, until the chutney is a thick, pulpy consistency. Taste and adjust with a pinch of sugar or drop of vinegar.

Spoon the chutney into the sterilised jar and immediately cover with the lid. Label and store in a cool, dark place for at least two months before eating.

To make the pâté marinade, put a small saucepan on a high heat and place all the marinade ingredients in the pan. Bring to the boil and reduce the liquid by a third. Remove the pan from the heat and set aside to cool. Once cool, place all the diced meats in a large bowl and pour over the marinade. Mix together well, cover and refrigerate overnight.

When you are ready to prepare the pâté, preheat the oven to 150°C/300°F/Gas 2. Divide the marinated meat mixture into four batches and put the meat into a food processor, a batch at a time. Chop the meat for 20–30 seconds, until it is the texture of coarse mince. Using a spatula, transfer the meat from the processor into a large mixing bowl.

Add the egg and pistachios and mix well with a large spoon to ensure all the ingredients are evenly combined.

Line the base of the terrine mould with a strip of greaseproof paper cut to fit the base. Tip the pâté mixture into the terrine mould and, with the edge of a spoon, press and pack the meat into the mould.

Tap the base of the terrine mould a couple of times on a work surface to ensure the meat is well pressed and contains no air gaps. On the top of the mixture press a bay leaf and a couple of sprigs of thyme. Cover the meat mixture loosely with a piece of buttered greaseproof paper, butter-side down. The paper should be cut neatly to fit inside the terrine mould and lie gently on the surface of the pâté. This will protect the pâté from the direct heat of the oven, so preventing it from discolouring and developing a crust.

Place the terrine mould into a bain-marie and slide onto the oven shelf. Carefully pour boiling water into the bain-marie until it reaches two-thirds of the way up the side of the terrine. Cook in the oven for 50 minutes. The inside of the pâté should have reached a temperature of between 65 and 70°C. If you have a temperature probe, use this to check. Remove the terrine from the oven and allow to cool at room temperature for 2 hours. When cooled, wrap in clingfilm and refrigerate for two days to let the flavours grow and mature.

To remove the pâté from the mould, slide the blade of a sharp knife against the side of the terrine and then tap the pâté onto a tray to free it. Carve into generous slices and serve with the matured spiced plum chutney. Eat with gherkins, pickles and lots of crusty bread.

ROAST LOIN OF PORK
STUFFED *with* DRIED PLUMS

A classic Maman Blanc dish that I used to enjoy as a Sunday roast. Two ingredients that love each other, the plum and sweetness of pork is a classic combination embraced by many cultures. The drying of the plums intensifies their flavour and removes the excess moisture. Like all great home-cooking, this recipe doesn't use stock. Ask your butcher to bone the loin, score the skin in a 5mm lattice and chop the bones in to small pieces for you for you. *Raymond Blanc*

Serves 6–8

8–10 Victoria plums, halved and stoned	1 large beef tomato, pricked with a fork all the way round
1.2kg pork loin	4 garlic cloves, unpeeled
salt and pepper	2 sprigs of thyme
30ml rapeseed oil	250ml water
400g pork bones	100ml Madeira, boiled for 30 seconds
50ml vegetable oil	(optional)

To dry the plums, preheat the oven to 100°C/200°F/Gas ¼. Place the plums halves on a tray and put in the oven for 2 hours. This can be done two days in advance and the plums kept in a container in the fridge.

Preheat the oven to 220°C/425°F/Gas 7. Open up the pork loin and flatten it onto the table, fat-side down. Season and place three-quarters of the dried plums along the middle of the loin, chop the remaining plums and reserve for the sauce. Roll the loin up and secure both ends tightly with skewers, tie with four turns of string. Remove the skewers.

In a small heavy-duty roasting pan, on a medium heat, colour the pork bones and meat trimmings in the rapeseed oil for 7–10 minutes until lightly golden and take off the heat.

In a large non-stick frying pan, on a medium heat, crisp the pork loin, skin-side down in the vegetable oil for 7–8 minutes, rolling the joint to ensure all the skin makes contact with the pan. Put the bones in a roasting tray and sit the pork on top. Add the tomato, garlic and thyme and roast in the oven for 30 minutes. Add the water and Madeira, if using, to create the jus. Turn down the oven to 180°C/350°F/Gas 4, cover the tin loosely with foil and cook for a further 35 minutes. Once cooked, add 100ml of water to lengthen the jus if needed. Place the loin on a plate and allow to rest for 30 minutes.

Tip the roasting tray slightly and spoon out half of the fat. Strain the remaining jus through a fine sieve into a medium casserole, heat and add the chopped plums. Taste to season, set aside and keep warm.

Cut away the strings and carve into 8–10 slices. Pour juices released from the meat into the sauce. Arrange the pork on a warm serving dish and pour on the juice and dried plums. Serve with summer vegetables and wild mushrooms as an alternative to a traditional roast.

PLUM, SHORTBREAD *and* SABAYON

This dessert is spectacular in looks, taste and texture. For this dish I use the sweet and yellow fleshed Victoria plums, barely cooked in their own juices. The contrast of the crumbly textured shortbread biscuit and gently cooked Victoria plums, gives the dish texture and flavour as well as a generous helping of this wonderful British fruit. This recipe produces more dough than you need, but the excess can be rolled, cut ready to bake, and kept in the freezer for up to one month. *Raymond Blanc*

Serves 4

Sabayon
4 free range egg yolks
125ml Muscat or sweet dessert wine
50g caster sugar
15ml lemon juice

Plums
16 Victoria plums, halved and stoned
50g caster sugar
10ml plum alcohol

juice of ¼ lemon

Shortbread
2 free range egg yolks
160g caster sugar
225g plain flour
7g baking powder
5g sea salt
160g unsalted butter, softened

Sabayon is best made one day in advance. In a bowl, whisk egg yolks, wine, sugar and lemon juice for one minute. Place the bowl over a bain-marie of barely simmering water and whisk for 7–8 minutes until a temperature of 78°C is reached and the sabayon is light and fluffy. Then whisk the bowl over crushed ice to chill. Refrigerate overnight.

Put the plums, sugar, alcohol and lemon juice into a bowl and leave to macerate. After an hour, cut 8 plum halves into quarters and set aside. Put the remaining plums in a pan and bring to a boil. Remove, add the quartered plums and allow to cool to room temperature.

To make the shortbread, put the egg yolks and sugar in the bowl of a kitchen mixer and, using the paddle attachment on high speed, mix together for 4 minutes until white and doubled in volume. Reduce the speed to minimum, add the flour, baking powder and salt and mix for 2 minutes. Add the butter and mix for 1 minute on medium speed. Scrape the dough onto a tray lined with greaseproof paper, cover with clingfilm and place in the fridge for 30 minutes for the dough to stiffen.

Preheat the oven to 160°C/310°F/Gas 2½. Between two sheets of greaseproof paper, roll out the dough to a thickness of 2mm. Place the dough in the freezer for 15 minutes. Remove the top layer of paper and cut the dough into four rectangles, each 5 x 15cm, and place on an oven tray. Put in the oven for 6 minutes until golden. Remove and trim the edges of the warm rectangles to a neat finish. Set aside and allow to cool on the tray.

To serve, place the plums halves together to reform whole plums. Place a shortbread biscuit on each plate and top with three plums. Spoon the quartered plums around each biscuit and serve with a spoonful of sabayon, dust twice with icing sugar and caramelise with a blow torch.

PLUM *and* ALMOND TART

Serves 4–6

Pastry	*Filling*
150g plain flour	150g butter, at room temperature
pinch of salt	150g sugar
75g unsalted butter, very cold, cut into small pieces	150g blanched almonds, finely chopped
40g icing sugar	20g plain flour
3 free range egg yolks	2 free range eggs
flour, for dusting	250g plums, halved and stoned

You will need a 23cm tart tin.

To make the pastry, sift the flour into a bowl with the salt. Add the butter and, using a food processor or the tips of your fingers, rub together until the mixture resembles rough breadcrumbs. Sift in the sugar and mix briefly, then add the egg yolks. Bring everything together with your hands to form a firm dough.

When the dough just holds together, wrap it in clingfilm and pat it into a large disc shape and rest in the fridge for at least 30 minutes.

In a bowl beat the butter and sugar together until pale and creamy. Add the chopped almonds and the flour and mix well. Then add the eggs, mixing again to make a paste. Scoop into a bowl and refrigerate.

Preheat the oven to 170°C/325°F/Gas 3. On a lightly floured surface, roll out the pastry to fit the tart tin. Gently ease the pastry into the tin, pressing it gently into the sides and corners. Trim off any excess. Place the pastry case in the fridge to rest for another 15 minutes.

Take out of the fridge and bake the pastry case in the oven for about 20 minutes or until the pastry has a firm, sandy texture. Remove and cool slightly.

When the pastry feels cool, spoon in the almond filling, spreading evenly. Place the plums, cut-side down, in circles on top of the filling and press in gently. Put in the oven and cook for about 40 minutes, or until the filling feels firm to the touch. Serve with crème frâiche.

PLUM JAM

Makes 4	1kg plums, stalks removed, halved and stoned
large jars	800g sugar
	juice of ½ lemon

You will need four large or six small sterilised jam jars with tightly fitting lids.

In a large, heavy-bottomed pan, put the plums, sugar and lemon juice and allow to stand for at least 30 minutes.

Meanwhile, to sterilise the jars, wash and dry thoroughly and, along with the lids, place upside down in an oven set at 150°C/300°F/Gas 2 for 10 minutes. Remove to a clean place and allow to cool. At the same time put a china saucer in the fridge to cool; you will need this to test the consistency of the jam later.

Bring the pan with the plums to a boil, stirring occasionally to prevent sticking. When the mixture begins to bubble, scoop off any scum that comes to the surface. Continue to cook the plums at a rolling boil for at least 10 minutes, stirring frequently.

To test if the jam is ready, put a drop on the cold saucer. If it sets quickly, it is ready. Otherwise continue to cook and test regularly until it sets.

Remove from the heat, spoon into the jars and seal immediately.

This will keep well in a cool, dry place for up to a year.

RHUBARB
with RECIPES *by* GREGG WALLACE

As we know, rhubarb is technically a vegetable, but the beauty of this wonderful plant is that it can be used in both sweet and savoury dishes. It has a fantastic tart acidity, which tastes just as good with sweet flavours, such as meringue or ice cream as it does with rich or oily ones like roast pork or smoked eel.

Early or forced rhubarb is grown in West Yorkshire from December to March, in an area known as the Rhubarb Triangle. It is a perfect bridge between the last of the autumn fruit and the beginning of the spring crops. 'Champagne' is one of the first varieties to arrive in the shops; beautiful slim stalks of delicate, almost iridescent pink. By April, the outdoor rhubarb has started to spring up in other parts of the country, thicker stalks, which vary in colour from green to pink-red with which to make puddings and jams or freeze for the rest of the year.

So if rhubarb is so good, what is happening to our production? During both world wars, rhubarb was one of the cheapest and most widely available foods, even being subsidised by the government so that people had access to it. It was relatively easy to produce and has great health benefits, including anti-bacterial and blood-purifying effects. However, since the 1950s, imported fruit alternatives have come into the market, causing rhubarb sales to fall into decline.

Now is the time for rhubarb's revival. It's time to make proper use of it in the kitchen, use it as a vegetable in a salad with creamy goat's cheese or spiced in chutney to serve with gammon. It is delicious sweetened and baked with ginger and gooseberries or used to make glorious puddings such as rhubarb meringue tart or trifle. By enjoying rhubarb in these many ways, we will protect our wonderful British heritage.

RHUBARB *and* GOAT'S CHEESE SALAD

This is a clever, but ridiculously easy recipe. It allows the rhubarb to be eaten recognisably sweet, whilst still serving it as an unconventional savoury dish. The rhubarb cooks in seconds, retaining its vivid colour. It is a very pretty salad and proves rhubarb's versatility. I wanted to serve rhubarb in a savoury dish, but at the same time show how pretty it can be. *Gregg Wallace*

Serves 1   60g butter
               4 tsp sugar
               100g rhubarb, cut into batons
               4 tsp port
               1 tbsp extra virgin olive oil
               1 tsp lemon juice
               1 tsp mustard
               salt and pepper
               baby salad leaves
               50g British hard goat's cheese, crumbled

Melt the butter in a frying pan and then add the sugar. Place the rhubarb in the pan and cook quickly until just tender. Remove the rhubarb from the pan and set aside to cool.

Deglaze the frying pan with the port, let the glaze cool and reserve to use later.

Mix the olive oil, lemon juice and mustard and season to taste. Make a loose ball of the leaves in the palm of your hand and place in the centre of a plate and dress with the olive oil mixture.

Make criss-cross patterns around the leaves with the rhubarb batons, sprinkle the goat's cheese over and around the rhubarb and finish with a drizzle of the port glaze.

GAMMON
with SPICED RHUBARB CHUTNEY

Once again we have lots of rhubarb and we're still nowhere near a dessert. Chutneys are not difficult to make, this spice and rhubarb flavour balance is my own, but I do urge you at another time to play with your rhubarb, add a little of the spices that you love, taste, add and taste again. Chutney allows you to personalise your rhubarb. Once you've made it, it becomes a spicy friend in the kitchen. It can be used to enliven many dishes, from a slice of Cheddar through to cured meats and griddled cuts. *Gregg Wallace*

Serves 2
500g rhubarb
200g soft brown sugar
3 onions, finely chopped
3 garlic cloves, chopped
100g tomatoes, chopped
1 tbsp thyme leaves
200ml red wine vinegar
zest and juice of 1 lemon
1 tsp ground ginger
½ tsp cinnamon
1 clove
2 gammon steaks
1 tbsp olive oil

Place the rhubarb, sugar and a splash of water in a pan and cook on a medium heat until soft. Add the onions, garlic, tomatoes and thyme, plus the vinegar, lemon zest and juice, and spices. Bring slowly to the boil, stirring occasionally. Then simmer for about 2 hours, stirring frequently, until the chutney is thick.

Cut through the gammon fat in several places with a pair of scissors.

Put the olive oil in a pan on a medium heat, and when the pan is hot, fry the gammon for 3–4 minutes on either side.

Place the gammon and some of the rhubarb chutney on plates and serve with cooked green cabbage.

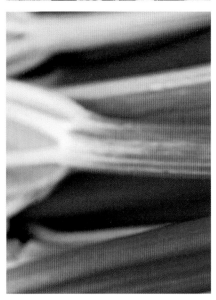

RHUBARB MERINGUE TARTS

Oh my word, this is a truly thrilling piece of culinary art. If, like me, you have a fondness for sweet things, you will be in heaven. I love slicing through this tart and gazing at the layers, white meringue atop, toasty base below and shiny rhubarb in the middle. This recipe is so achievable and the results are bordering majestic. Dessert, most certainly, or afternoon tea, this is unashamed cooking to impress. *Gregg Wallace*

Serves 4	300g sweet shortcrust pastry
	flour, for dusting
	butter, for greasing
	3 free range eggs, separated
	700g rhubarb, cut into 2cm chunks
	260g caster sugar
	juice and zest of 1 lemon
	5 tbsp cornflour
	4 tbsp water

You will need four 12cm flan tins.

Preheat the oven to 190°C/375°F/Gas 5. Roll out the pastry on a floured surface and use to line the greased flan tins. Prick the base of the pastry with a fork. Line the pastry with greaseproof paper and fill with baking beans, then bake blind for 10 minutes.

Take out of the oven, and remove the greaseproof paper and baking beans and brush the inside of the pastry cases using one of the egg yolks. Return to the oven and bake for a further 15 minutes until golden brown.

Put the rhubarb, 7 tablespoons of the sugar and the lemon juice and zest into a pan. Cover and cook on a low heat until the fruit has softened. Mash the fruit with a fork.

Mix the cornflour and water in a bowl until it forms a smooth paste. Stir into the rhubarb, bring to the boil, and stir until thick. Take off the heat and stir in the remaining two egg yolks. Use a ladle to pour the filling into the pastry cases.

Whisk the egg whites in a large bowl until they form stiff peaks. Gradually add the remaining sugar, whisking between each addition.

Pipe the meringue over the fruit filling. Bake for about 20 minutes or until the meringue is golden brown.

RHUBARB SALAD
with SMOKED EEL *and* POTATOES

Serves 4   300g small waxy potatoes
olive oil, for dressing
3–4 rhubarb stalks, cut into 2cm long sticks
50ml white wine
1 tsp coriander seeds
2–3 black peppercorns
3 tsp sugar
3 tbsp good-quality white wine vinegar
6 tbsp extra virgin olive oil
salt and pepper
2 handfuls of leaves (rocket and mizuna work well)
1 small bunch of chervil or parsley, leaves picked from the stem
300g smoked eel, sliced into thick strips

Put the potatoes in a pan of salted water, bring to a boil and cook until just tender. Drain and rinse under cold, running water to cool slightly before slicing and dressing lightly in olive oil.

Preheat the oven to 180°C/350°F/Gas 4. Place the rhubarb in a baking dish with the wine, coriander seeds, peppercorns and sugar. Put in the oven and bake for about 10 minutes or until the rhubarb is just soft but still holding its shape. Allow to cool slightly.

In a bowl, mix the vinegar and oil. Season with salt and pepper.

Put the salad leaves, herbs and sliced potato into a bowl, mix and dress. To serve, put the dressed leaves, herbs and sliced potatoes into a serving bowl and place the eel strips and rhubarb on top.

BAKED RHUBARB
with GOOSEBERRIES *and* CARDAMOM

Serves 6

1kg rhubarb, cut into short lengths
1kg gooseberries, topped and tailed
6 tbsp honey
4 tbsp elderflower cordial
1 tbsp stem ginger, chopped
8 cardamom pods, lightly crushed

Preheat the oven to 220°C/425°F/Gas 7. Put the rhubarb and gooseberries into a large baking dish. Pour over the honey and cordial and mix well. Sprinkle with the ginger and cardamom.

Place in the oven and bake for 20 minutes or until the rhubarb is soft but still retaining some of its shape and the gooseberries are soft and releasing their juice.

Delicious served with clotted cream and shortbread biscuits.

SIMPLE RHUBARB TRIFLE

Serves 4–6
500g rhubarb, cut into 3cm chunks
juice of 3 oranges
zest of 1 orange
2 tbsp caster sugar
100g flaked almonds
100g sponge fingers
5–6 tbsp sweet sherry
300ml double cream

Heat the oven to 150°C/300°F/Gas 2. Put the rhubarb, orange juice and zest and sugar into a baking dish. Bake for about 20 minutes or until the rhubarb is just soft. Remove and allow to cool.

While the oven is still hot, put the almonds on a baking sheet in the oven and toast for about 10 minutes, keeping an eye on them to make sure they don't burn.

Put the sponge fingers into a large glass bowl. Sprinkle over the sherry and allow to soak in for a couple of minutes. Meanwhile, whip the cream to form soft peaks.

Spoon the rhubarb and cooking juices over the soaked sponge fingers. Spread the cream over the top and sprinkle with the toasted almonds.

This can be eaten immediately, but is even better left for an hour or two in the fridge.

NUTS

with RECIPES *by* YOTAM OTTOLENGHI

In Ancient Greece and medieval Britain, doctors used walnuts to treat mental illness and headaches, believing that the nut's skull-like shell and brain-shaped kernel symbolised its magical curative powers. Now nuts have a very important place in cooking, giving flavour and texture to both sweet and savoury dishes. Crunchy salsas, or nutty sauces for smooth pasta, meringues flecked with hazelnuts or as a chunky, sweet brittle in ice cream. Not only are nuts very good for you and are even recommended to lower cholesterol, but they add vital flavour and bite to a dish.

Fresh nuts have an incredible flavour almost unrecognisable next to the dry, bitter imported varieties we have become used to, but sadly few of us experience them freshly harvested as we import most of the nuts we eat despite having varieties indigenous to our soil. So why are we not growing and eating our own produce in this country?

The cobnut is a cultivated variety of the British hazlenut and has been grown in the Garden of England since 1830. The most popular variety is the Kentish cob and it is in season to eat fresh between August and October when the nut is green. At the end of the season the nuts can be husked and dried and kept for the rest of the year.

The common walnut tree has been around for hundreds of years and the Victorians loved to pick walnuts, pickle them and then enjoy as a Christmas treat. Walnuts harvested green in early June for pickling are a true British delicacy or if left on the tree for their shells to harden, they are then harvested in September.

Sadly, with our taste for imported cashews and peanuts, the days of nut orchards in this country are almost gone. So to rediscover fabulous British nuts, look for cobnuts in late summer and early autumn and try to find walnuts grown in the UK or, if you can, plant a tree to harvest your own. Now is the time to reinstate the lost culture of enjoying these wonderful and delicious nuts.

ROASTED AUBERGINE
with WALNUT SALSA

Roasted aubergines and fresh walnuts make a beautiful combination, common in many areas around the Caspian and Black seas, particularly in countries like Georgia, Turkey and Iran. Here, pickled walnuts, a purely British food, are added. Their sweet sharpness is just what this dish needs to give it an extra kick. *Yotam Ottolenghi*

Serves 4

2 large aubergines
4 tbsp olive oil
coarse sea salt and black pepper
80g walnuts, chopped
60g pickled walnuts, chopped
1 tbsp walnut pickling liquid
2 tbsp cider vinegar

1 garlic clove, crushed
¼ tsp chilli flakes
2 tsp walnut oil
1 tbsp chopped parsley
1 tbsp chopped coriander
75g goat's cheese, crumbled
seeds of ½ pomegranate

Preheat the oven to 230°C/450°F/Gas 8. Cut both aubergines in half lengthways and score the flesh in a criss-cross pattern. Brush the flesh liberally with olive oil, making sure it soaks up a fair amount and then sprinkle with 1½ teaspoons of salt and some black pepper. Place on a baking tray, flesh-side up, and roast in the oven for about 40 minutes, until the flesh is cooked through and turns a dark golden-brown.

Meanwhile, make the salsa. In a small bowl, mix together the walnuts, walnut pickling liquid, vinegar, garlic, chilli, walnut oil, parsley and half the coriander, along with 1 teaspoon of salt.

Spoon the walnut salsa over the aubergines as soon as they come out of the oven and leave to cool completely. Sprinkle the remainder of the coriander on top before serving, along with the goat's cheese and pomegranate seeds.

MISO CHICKEN
with WALNUTS *and* GRAPES

This recipe is based on a popular dish served in my restaurant, NOPI, where we use quail rather than chicken. Whichever bird you choose to use, the quality of the walnuts is paramount. The fresher and sweeter they are, the better they will blend with grapes, giving just a light crunch and nutty flavour without taking over. *Yotam Ottolenghi*

Serves 4

8–12 free range chicken thighs, de-boned, skin left on
80g white miso paste
40g root ginger, finely grated
4 tbsp mirin
90ml cider vinegar
12 small shallots, peeled
1 tbsp sunflower oil

200ml white wine
90ml water
salt and white pepper
120g walnuts, broken
80g unsalted butter
1½ tbsp maple syrup
250g small, seedless red grapes
2 tbsp chopped tarragon

Place the chicken in a large bowl. Stir together the miso paste, ginger, mirin and 4 tablespoons of the cider vinegar and pour this over the chicken. Mix well, cover and leave in the fridge to marinate for at least 3 hours, or even better, for up to 24 hours.

Put the shallots in a saucepan and cover with water. Bring to the boil and cook for 5 minutes, until semi-soft. Drain and then cut the shallots in half, lengthways.

Preheat the grill to high. Lay the chicken out on a baking tray, skin-side up, along with all of the marinade and grill for 10 minutes.

As soon as the chicken goes under the grill, heat the sunflower oil in a sauté pan large enough to fit all of the chicken. Add the semi-cooked shallots and fry on a medium heat for 4 minutes, until browned. Add the remaining 2 tablespoons of cider vinegar and reduce for a few seconds. Pour in the wine, water, ½ teaspoon of salt and some white pepper and continue to cook for about 6 minutes.

Remove the chicken from the grill and add it to the pan, along with all of the juices. Stir gently and bring everything to a low simmer. Cover the pan and cook for 3–4 minutes, or until the chicken is just cooked.

Remove the chicken from the pan, keeping it somewhere warm, and add the walnuts, butter, maple syrup and grapes to the pan. Continue cooking and stirring until the butter emulsifies and the sauce thickens, about 2–3 minutes.

Serve the chicken with the sauce spooned on top, along with a sprinkle of tarragon.

FRUIT *and* COBNUT CRUMBLE CREAM

This is probably one of the most impressive ways you can find to finish a meal. The sweet spices, cardamom and star anise, tend to leave people speculating about the 'exotic flavours', while the intricate layers and caramelised nuts on top seal the majestic effect. *Yotam Ottolenghi*

Serves 4

4 small pears, peeled and
    cut into 2cm dice
2 tbsp lemon juice
4 ½ tbsp caster sugar
2 medium Bramley apples, peeled
    and cut into 2cm dice
16 blackberries
40g wholemeal flour
40g plain flour
50g unsalted butter, chilled and
    cut into 2cm cubes
25g soft brown sugar

pinch of salt
100g dried cobnuts or hazelnuts

Cream
150ml double cream
100ml Greek yogurt
100ml mascarpone cheese
1 tbsp caster sugar
½ tsp vanilla essence
½ tsp ground cardamom
½ star anise, ground

You will need a baking tray which snugly fits the pears and apples, and four large glasses or glass bowls.

Preheat the oven to 180°C/350°F/Gas 4. Mix the pears, lemon juice and 1 ½ tablespoons of caster sugar in a bowl. Spread out on the baking tray, cover with foil and place in the oven. After 10 minutes, add the apples, re-cover with the foil and return to the oven for 30 minutes. Remove and use a fork to crush the fruit together. Set aside to cool before folding in the blackberries.

To make the crumble, place both types of flour in a large mixing bowl with the butter, brown sugar and salt. Use your fingers to rub the mixture into a breadcrumb texture. Spread out on a parchment-lined baking tray and place in the oven for 15 minutes, until dry and cooked through. Remove and leave to cool.

Put the nuts and remaining caster sugar in a small saucepan and place on a medium heat. Cook for 5–10 minutes, stirring constantly with a wooden spoon, until the sugar dissolves and caramelises onto the nuts. Remove from the heat and spread out on a parchment-lined tray to cool. Roughly crush the nuts with the flat side of a large knife, or in a bowl with the end of a rolling pin, and set aside.

For the cream, place all of the ingredients in a large mixing bowl and whisk to soft peaks, taking care not to over-whip (it is quite thick to start with so shouldn't take more than 30 seconds).

To assemble, spoon two-thirds of the crumble into the bottom of the serving glasses. Cover the crumble with two-thirds of the nuts, fruit compote and the cream. The remaining third of the crumble goes on top of this, followed by the remaining third of the compote, the cream and finally the last of the nuts. Serve at once, or chill for a few hours before serving. If chilling, hold off sprinkling on the last third of the nuts until just before serving.

WALNUT *and* PARSLEY TAGLIATELLE

Serves 4
200g shelled walnuts
3 tbsp olive oil
1 garlic clove, crushed to a paste with salt
1 tbsp grated Parmesan, plus extra to serve
knob of butter
1 large handful of parsley, chopped
salt and pepper
1 tbsp cream
300g tagliatelle

Put the walnuts into a bowl and pour over boiling water. Leave for a minute and then drain. Peel away as much of the skins as you can and put the peeled walnuts into a blender or pestle and mortar.

Add the olive oil, garlic paste and Parmesan and crush together to make a thick paste. Add the butter and parsley and mix to make a green-flecked sauce. Season with salt and pepper and finally add the cream to loosen the mixture.

Bring a large pan of salted water to the boil and cook the tagliatelle until *al dente*. Drain away all the cooking water except for 4–5 tablespoons. Add the reserved water to the walnut paste and mix to make a sauce.

Toss the sauce with the tagliatelle and add extra Parmesan and olive oil before serving.

HAZELNUT BRITTLE ICE CREAM

Serves 6

Ice cream
450ml double cream
150ml full-fat milk
1 vanilla pod, seeds scraped out
5 free range egg yolks
50g caster sugar

Hazelnut brittle
50g hazelnuts, roughly chopped
100g caster sugar
100ml water

Put the cream and milk into a saucepan with the vanilla seeds. Heat until it is just starting to simmer. Remove and set aside.

Put the egg yolks and sugar into a large bowl and whisk for a couple of minutes until pale and creamy. Slowly pour the heated cream in a steady stream onto the yolk mixture, whisking all the time. (Incorporating extra air like this will make a lighter, fluffier ice cream.)

Return the mixture to the saucepan and cook very gently for a couple of minutes so that it thickens slightly. Pour into a shallow container to cool.

To make the hazelnut brittle, lay a large sheet of greaseproof paper in a shallow metal tray, overlapping the sides. Scatter the chopped nuts into the tray.

Place the sugar and water in a saucepan over a medium heat. When the sugar has melted, increase the heat and cook for a couple of minutes or until it starts to darken and caramelise. Remove from the heat and pour into the prepared tray, over the nuts. Set in a cool place to harden.

When it has hardened and cooled slightly, wrap the paper around the brittle and remove from the tray. Then, still wrapped in the paper, place the brittle on a hard surface and lightly crush with a rolling pin to break into little pieces.

Put the cooled ice cream mixture into the freezer and, every 15 minutes or so, give it a whisk or a stir to break up the ice crystals as it freezes. This will give the ice cream a creamier texture. When it is nearly solid, stir the brittle pieces through the ice cream. Return to the freezer to freeze completely. This will keep happily for up to a week in the freezer but is best eaten in the first couple of days.

FLOURLESS CHOCOLATE
and HAZELNUT CAKE

Serves 4   200g dark, bitter chocolate
125g butter
100g toasted hazelnuts, skins roughly rubbed off
1 tsp vanilla essence
4 free range eggs
125g caster sugar
icing sugar, for dusting

You will need a 20cm springform cake tin, buttered and lined with baking paper.

Preheat the oven to 180°C/350°F/Gas 4. Put the chocolate and butter into a heatproof bowl and place over a pan of boiling water. Melt together until smooth. Remove from the heat.

In a food processor, chop the hazelnuts to a fine powder. Pour the chocolate mixture into a larger bowl. Stir in the hazelnuts and vanilla essence and allow to cool slightly.

Beat together the eggs and sugar until very thick and creamy. Pour into the hazelnut and chocolate mix. Carefully fold together until all the chocolate is incorporated.

Spoon the mixture into the prepared cake tin and bake on the middle shelf of the oven for 45 minutes or until an inserted skewer comes out almost clean. Remove and allow to cool.

Carefully remove the cake from its tin; being flourless it will be quite fragile. It should have a crisp top but be soft and moist inside.

Delicious served with crème fraîche or whipped cream and fresh berries.

BEETROOT
with RECIPES *by* ANTONIO CARLUCCIO

Deep purple, candy pink, blush red and stripy golden – beetroot comes in an astonishing array of colours. It is full of natural sweetness, which tastes excellent combined with flavours like salty feta cheese or capers, fragrant fresh herbs or ripe tomatoes. Freshly pulled from the ground, beetroot has a sweetness and intensity you can rarely taste with imported varieties.

Beetroot is wonderful roasted whole or puréed into smooth soups, as well as raw in health-boosting juices or for a more indulgent innovation, baked in a beetroot chocolate cake. Beetroot eaten in these ways is a very different experience from eating it pre-cooked or pickled. Even the plant's leaves can be eaten; try cooking them like spinach in boiling water and dressing with olive oil and lemon. Bull's Blood is a variety especially suited to growing for its young, tender leaves which can be used raw in salads.

This beautiful-coloured root crop also contains large amount of nitrates and is packed with vitamins providing numerous health benefits as well as exercise performance-enhancing capabilities.

So why have we lost interest in this delicious vegetable? In the last few decades, we have lost almost half of our beetroot fields in the UK. Carrots, potatoes and other root crops have taken its place in our kitchens and heritage varieties such as Burpee's Golden are being forgotten, despite beetroot being perfectly suited to the British climate and an easy crop to grow.

Look for beetroot grown in the UK, or best, locally to where you are. Check they are still firm, as the fresher it is, the less time it will take to cook. It's time to give your plate some colour and enjoy the health-giving benefits of this underrated vegetable.

BEETROOT SOUFFLÉ
with ANCHOVY SAUCE

In Italian it is called *Soffiata* but in English, soufflé. The sweetness from the beetroot matches wonderfully with the savoury from the anchovy sauce, presenting you with a little challenge for the taste buds and a wonderful colour for the eyes. *Antonio Carluccio*

Serves 6

Beetroot soufflé
400g cooked beetroot, peeled and diced
160ml pink grapefruit juice
1 tsp hot horseradish
salt and pepper
3 tbsp plain flour
4 free range eggs, separated
20g butter, for greasing
20g fine dry breadcrumbs, for dusting

Anchovy sauce
125g unsalted butter
1 large garlic clove, cut into 3
10 anchovy fillets in oil, drained
100ml double cream

You will need six individual ramekin dishes.

Preheat the oven to 220°C/425°F/Gas 7. Put the beetroot, half of the grapefruit juice, horseradish, salt and plenty of pepper into a blender and blend until smooth.

Heat up the other half of the juice, mix with the flour to form a paste and add to the blender. Add the eggs yolks to the mixture one at a time and blend well until everything is smooth. Pour from the blender into a large bowl.

Whisk the egg whites until stiff and then carefully fold into the mixture.

Grease the ramekins with the butter and then dust with the breadcrumbs. Place the ramekins on a baking tray, pour the soufflé mix into each ramekin and bake in the oven for 20–25 minutes.

For the anchovy sauce, put the butter and garlic in a pan, fry together for 1 minute and then discard the garlic. Lower the heat and add the anchovy fillets. When they have dissolved to a cream, add the double cream. Stir to mix and remove from the heat.

With a spoon, make a hole in the middle of each hot soufflé and pour in 2 tablespoons of the sauce. Serve immediately.

BEETROOT LAYER BAKE

The idea to do this layered dish replacing the lasagne pasta with sliced beetroot came straight into my mind when thinking of this recipe. The smoked ham matches wonderfully with the beetroot and the béchamel sauce, engaging every one of your taste buds. *Antonio Carluccio*

Serves 4

400g beetroot
4 tbsp olive oil
1 tsp English mustard
100g leek, finely chopped
50g butter
1 tbsp flour
425ml milk
nutmeg, grated
black pepper
100g mature Cheddar cheese, grated
200g smoked roasted ham, cut into strips
Parmesan, grated

Preheat the oven to 180°C/350°F/Gas 4. Boil the beetroot in slightly salted water, peel and cut into 3mm slices. Place the beetroot into a bowl and mix with 2 tablespoons of the olive oil and the mustard. Fry the leek in 2 tablespoons of olive oil until soft.

In a saucepan melt the butter, stir in the flour and then add the milk in a steady stream until it is all incorporated. Add a grating of nutmeg and black pepper. Add the Cheddar and finally the leeks. Mix well and remove from the heat.

Put a layer of beetroot in the bottom of an ovenproof dish, spoon over the sauce, followed by a layer of ham. Repeat to build the layers and finish with a layer of the sauce and then sprinkle with Parmesan. Place in the oven and cook for 20 minutes until golden and bubbling.

PANNA COTTA
with BEETROOT *and* LIME SYRUP

Panna cotta, as we know, has become a hugely popular dish worldwide and has been made in lots of different ways. Adding the lime syrup and assorted coloured cubed beetroot makes this a delight to look at and a truly mouth-watering experience. *Antonio Carluccio*

Serves 4

Panna cotta
3 small gelatine leaves
250ml double cream
50ml milk
150g sugar
1 tbsp dark rum
1 tsp vanilla essence

Lime syrup
150g sugar
zest of 1 lime, cut into very small strips
juice of 2 limes
1 tbsp water

Beetroot
2 golden or red beetroot, cooked, peeled
and cut into small cubes

You will need four ramekin dishes.

Put the gelatine leaves into a bowl of cold water to soften.

Put the cream and milk into a small saucepan and bring to a boil. Add the sugar and softened gelatine and allow to dissolve. Pour in the rum and vanilla essence and stir. Remove from the heat and divide between the ramekins. Place in the fridge to chill for 2–3 hours.

To make the syrup, heat the sugar, lime zest and juice, and water in a pan until all the sugar has dissolved and the syrup is transparent. Take off the heat and allow to cool.

To loosen the panna cottas, dip each ramekin into hot water for just a few seconds, then turn upside down and gently release onto a serving plate.

Decorate each panna cotta with the cooked beetroot cubes and spoon over the lime syrup.

BEETROOT, TOMATO *and* HERB SALAD

Serves 4   400g mixed coloured beetroot, cleaned
2–3 sprigs of thyme
1 tsp salt
400g large ripe tomatoes
½ bunch each of mint, parsley and basil,
  leaves picked from the stem and roughly chopped

Dressing
½ garlic clove, crushed to a paste with salt
1 tbsp good-quality red wine vinegar
3 tbsp olive oil
sea salt and pepper

Put the beetroot into a saucepan with the thyme, cover with cold water and add a teaspoon of salt. Bring to the boil and cook until tender. Drain and leave to cool before slipping off the skins.

Slice the the cooled beetroot and tomatoes into thick slices.

Make the dressing by placing the crushed garlic, red wine vinegar and olive oil in a bowl or jug. Whisk thoroughly and season with salt and pepper.

When you are ready to serve, put the beetroot and tomatoes in a bowl. Add the herbs to the dressing and mix well. Pour over the beetroot and tomatoes. Season well and toss to coat.

ROASTED BEETROOT
with ROASTED GARLIC
and HORSERADISH

Serves 4–6   500g beetroot, scrubbed clean and halved
olive oil
1 head of garlic, cloves peeled
2 tbsp grated fresh horseradish
1 bunch of thyme, leaves picked from the stem
sea salt and pepper

Preheat the oven to 200°C/400°F/Gas 6. In a large baking tray, mix the beetroot with the oil, garlic, horseradish and thyme and season well. Cover tightly with foil and roast for 30 minutes.

Remove the foil and continue to roast for another 20 minutes until the beetroot is crisp on the outside, feels soft when a skewer is inserted and the garlic cloves are soft and sweet.

This is excellent with roast meats as a vegetable side dish.

COCKLES *and* MUSSELS
with RECIPES *by* VALENTINE WARNER

'Cockles and mussels, alive, alive, oh,' sang Molly Malone as she wheeled her barrow through the streets of Dublin. That may have been in Ireland, but in this country too, not too many years ago, eating a pint of this delicious fresh seafood was as natural as buying the day's newspaper.

These little bivalves are our own fantastic, natural resource. Mussels are sustainably fished, quick to cook and packed with vitamins and minerals. Many of these wonderful creatures come from the Scottish, Welsh or Norfolk coasts, and have done for hundreds of years. A mussel fishery on the River Conwy in North Wales was recorded as early as the eleventh century.

This island nation has an abundance of seafood but we have stopped buying and eating it as much as we used to. Cockles and mussels, clams and whelks are all harvested in huge quantities by British fisheries. But we now export more than 60% of our catch only to then import tinned, frozen or live mussels back. If the French and Spanish import our mussels because they like them so much, why aren't we eating them?

Cockles were traditionally hand-picked and sold by volume not weight and bought by the pint glass. Now you can buy live cockles in their shells. When you get them home, shake them under cold, running water to remove grit and expose any glued together with silt. Steam them as you would mussels and then add vegetables such as celery, fennel, garlic, leeks or onions. Adding diced bacon is good too and a little white wine or cider, and then watch until they pop open. Drain the liquor through a very fine sieve and use this as a base for a delicious sauce. Cockles taste fantastic in risottos, pastas (our version of spaghetti alle vongole), fish stews or surf and turf style with chicken. Due to their abundance on the Welsh coast, a wide range of cockle recipes, many ancient, come from that region (including *cocos ac wyau* – a.k.a. cockles and eggs).

Mussels have beautiful blue-black shells which contain the juicy flesh. Steam them open with wine or cider and serve in deep bowls with a spoon for the liquor and lots of bread. The Belgians eat them with chips; the French make their famous moules marinière; the Italians cook them with sweet, ripe tomatoes; the Spanish put them in paella and the Turks like to eat them stuffed and baked.

So now it's our turn to enjoy this wonderful supply of delicious fresh seafood, harvested from our coastline. You'll be supporting our marine environments, our fishing communities and eating something wonderful.

STUFFED MUSSELS

This is a great recipe to serve up if a fair few guests are coming and time is short, the perfect pre-dinner nibble. Alone with the telly, it is the snack of kings. It is probably worth doubling up the amounts as they tend to disappear quickly and this is good as they are better hot. If nuts threaten your wellbeing then by all means leave them out. Hazelnuts work as well in the recipe in place of walnuts for those that can eat them. It is imperative to only just cook the mussels when steaming them, as they will be cooked a second time under the grill.
Valentine Warner

Serves 6

24 large live mussels, de-bearded and cleaned
1 large banana shallot, finely chopped
75g unsalted butter, softened
50ml Martini
2 garlic cloves, crushed
30–40g walnut halves, smashed or chopped into small pieces
zest of 1 lemon, finely grated plus the juice of ½
25g Parmesan, finely grated
50g fresh breadcrumbs
2 tbsp very finely chopped parsley
½ tbsp very finely chopped tarragon
salt and freshly ground black pepper, to taste
rock salt, to scatter

You will need a large baking tray.

Preheat the grill to a moderate to high heat. Discard any mussels that are broken or that don't close when tapped. Tip the good, closed mussels into a pan with a splash of boiling water and cover with a tight-fitting lid. Cook over a high heat for 2 minutes or until only just opened and then pour into a large colander and leave to cool.

In a small pan, soften the shallot in 25g of butter and then pour in the Martini. Cook until it has evaporated and then scrape the softened shallot into a mixing bowl.

To make the stuffing, combine all the remaining ingredients with the shallots and season with plenty of freshly ground black pepper.

Remove and discard the top shell of the mussels. Add a teaspoon of the stuffing to each shell and arrange on a baking tray in rows. Put under the grill for 2–3 minutes or until golden brown and bubbling. To serve, transfer to a plate and scatter generously with rock salt as this will keep them stable on the plate. Eat with additional lemon if desired.

HEARTY WINTER MUSSELS

I remember the first time a large blue mountain of moules marinière was set before me. I was five, the table was high and the chair low. My vision was totally obscured from behind this tower and in its shadow; my father leant over and taught me to tease the plump orange meat from the shell by using another empty shell as tweezers. An unsqueamish little fellow, eyes wide with the genius of it all and I was in love from the first mouthful. From that point on my brother and I demanded mussels every day of that holiday for breakfast lunch and tea.

As much as I love this classic dish, sometimes I want something more luxurious and this recipe is comparable to being wrapped in a large woollen blanket or cuddled by mussels, excellent on a cold day – respite from a stinging wind and wet clothing. The pastis is the magic in the sauce. *Valentine Warner*

Serves 2   40g butter
2 medium banana shallots, finely diced
2 garlic cloves, finely chopped
2 celery sticks, finely chopped
1 bay leaf
50ml Pernod
1 tbsp plain flour
150ml milk
1kg live mussels, de-bearded and cleaned
300ml white wine
200ml double cream
crusty bread, to serve

Melt the butter in a small saucepan over a low heat and sauté the shallots, garlic, celery and bay leaf until softened but not coloured. Pour in the Pernod and continue to cook until it has evaporated.

Stir in the flour and gently cook out for minute or so. Slowly add the milk, a little at a time, stirring or whisking continuously to achieve a smooth, thick white sauce.

Meanwhile, tip the mussels and wine into a separate pan, cover with a lid and steam the mussels for 3–4 minutes until the shells have just opened.

Place a colander over the pan containing the white sauce and drain the mussel liquor into the sauce. Return the mussels to their pot and cover with a lid to keep warm.

Working quickly, whisk the mussel liquor into the white sauce and bring to the boil until it is the consistency of double cream. Gently stir in the cream and then pour the sauce into the pot of mussels. Serve immediately with crusty bread.

WELSH LAMB
with COCKLES

Personally I like surf and turf – clam chowder, steak and oysters, calves liver and scallops. Picture the Welsh lambs nibbling away on grasses with a sea view overlooking breezy wet sand where fat cockles nestle and bubble. The sweet salty cockle meat seasons and complements the tender lamb more than beautifully. Conveniently too, both ingredients are at their best come the later months of the year. Be sure to vigorously shake the cockles in a colander under cold running water to reveal any shells mudded together and prevent their dark designs spoiling the dish. Please try to use good old-fashioned tasting cider, not the pub-sold orange stuff that requires ice. *Valentine Warner*

Serves 4

600g cockles
300ml cider, medium sweet
3 lamb neck fillets
1 tsp thyme, finely chopped
salt and pepper
generous knob of butter
1 large onion, halved and finely sliced
100g lardons of bacon
generous splash of cider vinegar
1 tbsp curly parsley and celery leaves (if available), chopped

Preheat the oven to 170°C/325°F/Gas 3. Place the cockles in a colander and hold under a cold running tap, then shake to wash off any grit or break open any glued together with silt.

Put the cockles and cider into a medium-sized heavy pan. Cover with the lid and, while taking care not to overcook the cockles, steam for 2–3 minutes until all the shells have opened. Discard any which remain closed. Strain the cockles, using a fine sieve to remove as much grit as possible from the cockle liquor. Set aside both cockles and liquor.

Season the lamb with thyme, salt and pepper. In a very hot ovenproof pan, melt the butter and quickly brown the lamb all over to intensify the taste. Remove from the pan and set aside.

Tip the onion and bacon into the same pan and cook over a moderate heat until the onions are translucent. Pour in the cider vinegar and deglaze the pan. Return the lamb to the pan and pour in the cockle liquor. Cover the pan with a lid, place in the oven and cook for 45 minutes to 1 hour. Meanwhile, pick three-quarters of the cockles from their shells, leaving the rest with shells attached. When the lamb is tender, add all the cockles and warm through and then stir in the parsley.

Check the cooking liquor for seasoning and adjust. When ready, slice the lamb and ladle with the cockles and liquor onto plates and serve with boiled potatoes and savoy cabbage.

COCKLE *and* MUSSEL SOUP
with CROÛTONS

This soup can also be made with just mussels if cockles are hard to find, in which case, increase the quantity of mussels.

Serves 4

1kg mixed cockles and mussels
250ml dry white wine
2 tbsp olive oil
2 leeks, cleaned and finely sliced
salt and pepper
2 garlic cloves, finely sliced
2 tomatoes, peeled, deseeded
   and chopped
1 handful of parsley leaves,
   finely chopped

2–3 sprigs of marjoram,
   leaves picked and finely chopped
2 sprigs of thyme,
   leaves picked and finely chopped
500ml fish stock

Croûtons
olive oil, for frying
6 slices of white baguette

Give the cockles a good rinse in cold water and drain well. Discard any cracked ones.

To clean the mussels, scrub them well under running cold water, scraping off any barnacles and pulling away their dark beards. If any remain open or are broken or cracked, discard them.

Heat a large saucepan with a lid and put in the cockles and mussels. Pour over the wine and bring to the boil. Cook for about 3 minutes, lid on, shaking the pan from time to time. When all the mussels have opened, remove the cockles and mussels from the pan with a slotted spoon. Drain the wine through a sieve into a bowl and set aside.

In a clean saucepan, heat the oil and gently fry the leeks with a little salt until they become soft and sweet. Add the garlic and continue to cook for a minute or so before adding the tomato, herbs and some more salt. When the tomato has cooked a little and is starting to break up, pour in the strained wine and fish stock and simmer gently for 5 minutes.

While this is cooking, remove the cockles and mussels from their shells, throwing away the empty shells and any mussels that haven't opened. Add the cockles and mussels to the soup and cook for a minute or so.

To make the croûtons, heat some oil in a frying pan and fry the slices of bread until golden and crisp.

To serve, ladle the soup into bowls and slide a croûton into each bowl to absorb the juices.

MUSSEL SPAGHETTI

Serves 4–6   olive oil, for frying
3 garlic cloves, sliced
150ml white wine
3kg mussels, cleaned
1 handful of parsley, leaves picked from the stem and chopped
1 red chilli, deseeded and finely chopped
4 large tomatoes, peeled, deseeded and chopped
1 small bunch of marjoram, leaves picked from the stem and chopped
salt and pepper
200g spaghetti
extra virgin olive oil

Heat a couple of tablespoons of the olive oil in a large pan. Add half of the garlic and cook briefly before pouring in the wine. Allow the wine to heat to a boil before adding the mussels and parsley. Cover and cook for a couple of minutes or until the mussels open.

Drain the mussels from the wine using a sieve over a bowl, reserve the liquid and allow the mussels to cool.

Using the same pan, heat a little more oil and fry the rest of the garlic and chilli until the garlic just begins to colour. Add the chopped tomatoes and the marjoram and a good pinch of salt and some pepper. Cook together for 10 minutes or so, until the tomatoes start to reduce to a thick sauce.

While the sauce is cooking, remove the cooled mussels from their shells and taste the cooking liquid for seasoning. When the tomatoes have reduced, add the mussels and a few tablespoons of the cooking liquid to make a loose sauce.

Meanwhile, cook the spaghetti in plenty of boiling salted water until just *al dente*. Drain, return to the saucepan and add the mussel and tomato sauce. Add a good glug of extra virgin olive oil and check for seasoning. Toss well and cook the spaghetti in the sauce for 1 minute to absorb some of the sauce. It is now ready to serve.

PEAS
with RECIPES *by* AINSLEY HARRIOTT

The arrival of fresh peas in early summer signifies the beginning of our best vegetable season. These first tiny peas are tender and sweet and don't even need cooking. Just snap open the pod and pop them into your mouth or sprinkle them raw into salads. You can even add the tender shoots and tips of the plant to the salad leaves. This versatile vegetable has delicate-coloured and scented flowers and when the peas are harvested, the pods can be used in cooking to make broths or stocks.

Peas have a wonderful natural sweetness, which goes well with salty foods, such as pea and ham hock salad or soup with crisp prosciutto. They can be braised with garden lettuces to make a perfect summer side-dish or cooked to tenderness in a creamy risotto.

The garden pea has been grown in Britain since the sixteenth century. But over the last 100 years, 98% of pea varieties have become extinct. Out of 35,000 hectares of peas grown in Britain, only 3,000 hectares are sold as hand-picked podded peas for the fresh market, the rest are frozen. The fresh pea market is in serious decline and we're losing these heirloom vegetables which are part of our British heritage.

Before frozen peas were available, peas were harvested in the summer and dried for use throughout the year. Marrowfats were a cheap food, full of protein and fibre that would see people through the harsh winter months.

But now it's time to think about fresh peas, to look forward to the arrival of their summer season and make the most of them when they're at their peak. Find freshly-picked peas in the pod in farmers' markets or good supermarkets and make sure they're grown in Britain or, better still, if you have a chance to grow your own in a pot or small flower bed, you can buy seeds from the Heritage Seed Library and experiment with different varieties.

FRESH PEA, BROAD BEAN
and HAM HOCK SALAD

This salad is an all-time favourite. I don't know why ham hock ever went out of fashion – but I'm really pleased to see it back in the shops. Peas do something really great to ham. The saltiness of the meat and the sweetness of the peas are a fantastic combination. *Ainsley Harriott*

Serves 4
750g broad beans, podded
750g fresh peas, podded
200g mangetout, trimmed
3 tbsp extra virgin olive oil
1 tbsp cider vinegar
1 mild red chilli, deseeded and finely chopped
2 spring onions, trimmed and finely sliced
1 small bunch of flat-leaf parsley, roughly chopped
1 tbsp chopped fresh mint
180g pack of pulled ham hock
75g pack of pea shoot salad (optional)
sea salt and freshly ground black pepper

Bring a large pan of water to the boil, add the broad beans and cook for 2 minutes. Remove with a slotted spoon into a bowl of iced water to refresh. Re-boil the water and tip in the peas and mangetout. Cook for 1 minute, then drain and quickly refresh in a large bowl of iced water. Slip the broad beans out of their pods.

Drain and pat all the vegetables dry with kitchen paper and tip into a large bowl, then stir in the olive oil and cider vinegar.

Just before serving, stir the chilli, spring onions, parsley, mint and ham hock into the peas and beans, and toss in the pea shoots if using. Season to taste and serve immediately.

JERK PORK BELLY
with FRESH PEA *and* POTATO MASH-UP

Fresh pea and potato mash-up is a great side dish. Here I've paired it with one of my favourite cuts of pork subtly spiced with jerk seasoning and slowly roasted for a truly succulent eating experience. I like to serve it with a little hot Pickapeppa sauce on the side. *Ainsley Harriott*

Serves 6

Jerk pork belly
1.5kg pork belly, rind removed
1 tbsp dry jerk seasoning
300ml dry cider
475ml chicken stock
1 onion, sliced into 1cm rings
4 garlic cloves, sliced
4 sprigs of thyme
sea salt
freshly ground black pepper

Pea and potato mash-up
675g new potatoes, scraped
   or scrubbed
100ml extra virgin olive oil
225g peas (shelled weight)
sea salt
freshly ground black pepper

Preheat the oven to 180°C/350°F/Gas 4. Rub the pork belly all over with the jerk seasoning and place in a heavy-based frying pan, fat-side down. Cook for a few minutes until golden, then quickly sear on all sides to seal. Remove from the heat and leave to rest for about 5 minutes.

Pour the cider into a large jug with the chicken stock. Place the onion rings in a roasting tin and scatter with the garlic and thyme. Lay the rested pork belly on top and pour the cider mixture around the meat. Season to taste. Cover with foil and then braise for 2½–3 hours until the pork is tender and completely soft. Remove the foil.

Increase the heat of the oven to 220°C/425°F/Gas 7 and roast the meat for another 20–25 minutes until lightly crispy and golden brown. Leave to rest.

Meanwhile, place the potatoes in a large pan of salted water and bring to the boil. Cover and simmer for 12–15 minutes until tender, then drain well. Tip the cooked potatoes into a large bowl, and using the back of a fork, gently crush each potato until it just splits and then drizzle over the olive oil. Season and then mix carefully until all the oil has been absorbed.

Meanwhile, cook the peas in a separate pan of boiling salted water for 3–4 minutes until tender and then drain well. Mix through the crushed potatoes, and season to taste. Arrange the mash-up on plates with slices of jerk pork belly. Serve at once with some hot pepper sauce if you like.

FRESH PEA, COURGETTE
and PARMESAN RÖSTI
with TANGY TOMATO DRESSING

Fresh peas and courgettes – the taste of summer. As courgettes have a naturally high water content it is very important that they get squeezed dry before using them in this recipe. This will ensure that they are lovely and crisp. With the added texture of the ground rice, these really are a delicious rösti. *Ainsley Harriott*

Serves 4

Rösti

200g fresh peas (shelled weight)
350g courgettes, grated
150g ground rice
3 tbsp shredded basil leaves, plus extra to serve
75g Parmesan cheese, grated
50g pine nuts, lightly toasted
2 free range eggs, lightly beaten
salt
freshly ground black pepper
2 tbsp olive oil

Tangy tomato dressing

90ml olive oil
1 ripe plum tomato, deseeded and finely diced
4 sun-dried tomatoes in oil, drained and finely chopped
1 small shallot, finely chopped
1 tbsp red wine vinegar
salt
freshly ground black pepper

Blanch the peas in a pan of boiling salted water for 2 minutes until just tender, then drain and quickly refresh in a bowl of iced water and drain again. Squeeze the courgette as dry as possible in a clean tea towel and tip into a large bowl. Mix in the blanched peas, ground rice, basil, Parmesan and pine nuts. Then add the eggs, season to taste and mix to combine. Divide into 16 even-sized balls, then flatten slightly into rösti.

Heat 1 tablespoon of olive oil in a large non-stick frying pan on a medium heat and carefully add half of the rösti. Cook for 2–3 minutes on each side or until cooked through and crisp and golden. Drain on kitchen paper and keep warm. Repeat with another tablespoon of oil and the remaining rösti.

To make the dressing, place the olive oil, plum tomato, sun-dried tomatoes, shallot and vinegar in a bowl and season to taste. Stir until well combined.

Place a stack of rösti on each plate, and then drizzle a little dressing over and around the rösti and garnish with a sprinkling of shredded basil leaves.

PEA, PROSCIUTTO *and* MINT SOUP

Serves 4

20g butter
1 small shallot, finely chopped
200g podded peas (shelled weight)
small mixed bunch of mint and tarragon,
    removed from the stem and finely chopped
salt and pepper
1 tbsp cream
8 slices of prosciutto, chopped into small pieces

In a large saucepan, melt the butter and gently cook the shallot for a few minutes until soft but not brown. Add the peas and the chopped herbs and stir. Season well and cover with water. Bring to a simmer and cook for 5 minutes or until the biggest peas are soft.

Place the mixture into a blender and purée until smooth. Add the cream while the soup is still hot.

Just before serving, heat a frying pan and fry off the prosciutto pieces until crispy.

Serve the soup warm with the prosciutto sprinkled on top.

PEA RISOTTO

Serves 4–6

1 litre chicken stock
20g butter
1 large onion, finely chopped
sea salt and pepper
225g risotto rice
150g peas (shelled weight)
10g butter, to finish
½ small bunch of fresh tarragon, finely chopped
grated Parmesan

Bring the chicken stock to the boil in a pan.

In a heavy-bottomed saucepan, melt the butter and add the chopped onion and a little salt. Fry for several minutes until it is soft and sweet but not coloured. Increase the heat and add the rice, stirring well. Cook together for a minute before adding a ladle of the hot stock. Stir well, allowing the rice to absorb the stock before adding the next ladle. Continue to do this until a quarter of the stock has been added.

Tip in the peas and continue to cook in this way, adding the remaining stock and allowing it to absorb, until the peas are soft and the rice *al dente*. When the peas and rice are cooked, you should be left with a creamy, liquid sauce, much soupier than a normal risotto.

Add the butter and season well. Stir in the tarragon and Parmesan to serve.

BRAISED PEAS
with LITTLE GEM

This is a perfect summer side dish for for roast chicken.

Serves 4–6 as a side dish

50g butter, keeping aside 10g to finish
4 shallots, finely chopped
sea salt and pepper
500g peas (shelled weight)
8 Little Gem lettuces, quartered
300ml chicken stock
chopped herbs, to finish (parsley, mint or tarragon)

In a saucepan melt 40g of butter and sweat the shallots with a little salt, for several minutes until they are soft and sweet. Add the peas and the lettuce and continue to cook for a minute before adding the chicken stock. Season well.

Turn down the heat and simmer gently for about 20 minutes, shaking the pan every now and then to prevent sticking.

To finish, stir in the remaining butter and chopped herbs.

BEEF
with RECIPES *by* JOHN TORODE

Britain is famous for beef, we are even called 'les rosbifs' by our neighbours. Indeed, roast beef is our classic dish, but why are we not eating our own native breeds?

Many of our breeds are under threat. Most cattle raised in this country are not British pure-breed. Many originate from the Continent, brought in after World War II to meet increasing demand. We're losing special native cattle and a unique gene pool which is vital to the future of our country's food heritage.

So what makes rare breeds better? First of all, their quality of flavour and texture. Rare breeds take longer to mature so they have better marbling (or fat distribution), and properly produced beef is hung for longer which gives it a much deeper taste. Breeds to look out for are Dexter, Hereford, Longhorn, Shetland and White Park.

Cows are huge animals and there are many different cuts you can get from one beast, each with its own characteristic flavour and texture, and the better the quality, the better these cuts taste. What's more, the less popular cuts are good value. Skirt steak has a fantastic flavour and bite, try it grilled with mushrooms and tarragon. Chuck steak is an inexpensive shoulder cut and is superb cooked slowly in a Moroccan-style tagine with prunes. Shin has an excellent flavour and, braised until tender, makes a hearty weekend dish, or for a stunning Sunday lunch centrepiece, try a slow-roast, four-bone rib.

You can support our farmers who are trying to do this for us by buying their produce and learning about what really good beef tastes like. Try out different cuts of meat, get to know their special characteristics and understand how to cook them. Bring British beef back from the brink of extinction and enjoy much better flavour.

TOSCANA
with CHARRED SHALLOTS *and* THYME

This huge hunk of meat takes time. It has both the sirloin and the filet attached to the bone, and that means the best of both worlds, flavour with texture and tenderness and rich bloodiness, each one with the meat hanging freely but with plenty of fat.

I often cook this with all the fat so I get all the flavour and then trim some of the fat before I carve it. Because this is a big, well-used muscle, I do not believe that it should be too rare or it will be tough; the sinew and the fat need to break down. *John Torode*

Serves 6–8	2 x 24oz T-bone steaks, thickly-cut
	salt and pepper
	500g Swiss chard
	50ml vegetable oil
	12 banana shallots, peeled
	110g butter
	2 bay leaves
	sprig of thyme
	sea salt and pepper
	250ml beef or veal stock
	60g anchovies, chopped
	20g capers
	juice of 1 lemon

Preheat the oven to 220°C/425°F/Gas 7. Strip the leaves from the chard, wash and set to one side. Trim the stalks of any blemishes and cut into sticks about 5cm long and 2cm wide. To blanch the chard stems, bring a saucepan of lightly-salted water to the boil. Throw in the stalks and return to the boil. Drain and cool the stalks in cold water. Once refreshed, drain and set aside.

Heat the oil in a frying pan, add the shallots and colour them over a high heat. Once they have coloured, drain off and discard the oil. Add 50g butter, the bay leaves, thyme and salt to the pan. Cook for 5 minutes, turning and shaking the shallots, but try not burn the butter. Add enough stock to just cover the base of the pan and allow the liquid to reduce before adding more to the pan. As the liquid cooks the shallots, it will also reduce and become sticky. Continue until the shallots are cooked very soft and have a thick buttery and beefy glaze.

Meanwhile, heat a griddle plate and season the beef well – remember this is a thick cut! Score the fat a little and place the cutlets fat-side down on the griddle. The fat will start to melt and it's this fat which will flavour the outside of this great big beauty.

Once the fat is melting and starting to char, leave the beef to cook for 4 minutes. Turn it over and cook for another 4 minutes. Turn again but this time so that you rotate the meat and hold it in place with tongs to cook it on its narrower side for 2 minutes. Then flip over, hold in place and cook the other narrower side for 2 minutes. Take it off the griddle plate and put it into the hot oven for about 6 minutes for a medium steak.

Let it rest for 5 minutes before serving it whole … you have to show off!!!

While the steak is in the oven, heat a frying pan over a high heat and melt the rest of the butter. Add the blanched chard stalks, cook for 3 minutes and then add the leaves, stirring until they wilt. Season, add the anchovies, capers and lemon juice and cook for 2 minutes.

Using a slotted spoon, drain the chard and put onto warm large plates, reserving the sauce. Place the steak on the top of the chard and pour over the remaining buttery anchovy and caper sauce from the pan. Serve with a spoonful of caramelised shallots on each plate.

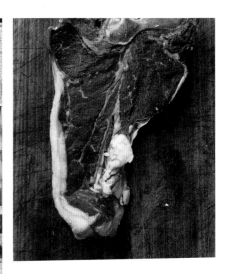

BRAISED SHIN OF BEEF
with PARSNIP PURÉE

The muscles that do the work on a bovine have a rich and deep flavour but need to be cooked long and slow. This beauty of a cut is my favourite as when it's been cooked for 2–3 hours it's sticky and soft and melts in your mouth…just the way great beef should be. *John Torode*

Serves 8–10

4kg beef shin, on the bone
salt and freshly ground black pepper
olive oil, for frying
2 carrots, chopped
1 onion, chopped
1 celery stalk, chopped
1 garlic clove, crushed
2 star anise
400ml red wine
100ml port
1 pig's trotter
300ml beef stock
425ml stout

4 tbsp dark soy sauce
2 tbsp fish sauce

Parsnip purée
1kg parsnips, peeled and
  cut into small cubes
2 shallots, finely chopped
200ml milk
100ml cream
2 bay leaves
olive oil
juice of ½ lemon
salt and white pepper

Preheat the oven to 190°C/375°F/Gas 5. Trim most of the excess fat from the shin, leaving some on for colour and flavour. Prepare the beef by taking the meat off the bone in seams and cut into big hunks. Season really well. Heat a little oil in a frying pan, add the pieces of beef and fry until well browned on all sides.

Heat some more oil in a heavy-based flameproof casserole. Add the vegetables and star anise and cook briefly until the vegetables are just soft. Pour in the red wine and port and bubble until reduced by half. Add the beef and trotter and cover with stock. Bring to the boil. Skim any scum from the surface and add the stout, soy sauce and fish sauce. Transfer to the oven and cook for 3 hours, or until the meat is very tender.

Take the casserole out of the oven, remove the meat from the pan and keep warm. Strain the cooking liquid, return to the pan and bring to the boil. Keep bubbling until the sauce is thick. Taste and season. Take the pig's trotter out of the sauce and reserve the meat – delicious on toast! Return the beef to the pan and put back in the oven for a further 30 minutes.

Meanwhile, to make the parsnip purée, put the parsnips and shallots into a saucepan with the milk, cream and bay leaves and cover with water. Add 1 tablespoon of olive oil, lemon juice and a good pinch of salt and bring to the boil. Reduce the heat and simmer gently for 15–20 minutes. Drain the vegetables, reserve the cooking liquid and discard the bay leaves. Put the parsnips and shallots into a food processor and turn on at low speed. Add white pepper and some of the vegetable cooking liquid until the purée is the consistency of whipped cream. Taste and season and keep hot.

When the beef is ready, spoon onto plates and serve with the parsnip purée.

SLOW ROAST FOUR-BONE RIB OF BEEF
with YORKSHIRE PUDDING

Ask your butcher to trim the beef, remove the chine bone (which is the flat bone attached to the rib) and to clean the bones ready for roasting, but keep the trimmings. The beef fat is great for roasting the potatoes in and if you ask your butcher to mince the remaining trim it makes great meatballs for nibbles. *John Torode*

Serves 10

5kg four-bone rib of beef, trimmed
100ml oil
salt and pepper
4 carrots halved

Crust
50g butter, plus extra for greasing
2 large onions, diced
300g white breadcrumbs
300g wholegrain mustard

200ml water
3 free range eggs
salt and pepper

Yorkshire pudding
8 free range eggs
600ml milk
½ tsp salt
500g plain flour
3 tbsp dripping

First thing in the morning, remove the beef from the fridge to come to room temperature. Rub it all over with the oil followed by the salt and pepper.

Preheat the oven to 220°C/425°F/Gas 7. To make the crust (this can be done the day before if you wish), melt the butter in a pan and fry the onions until tender. Put the breadcrumbs in a large bowl and in a smaller bowl mix the mustard and water together. Tip the onions into the breadcrumbs, add the mustard mix, the eggs, season well and mix everything together to make a paste.

Spread the paste evenly over the beef, leaving the ends uncovered. Cover the paste with well-greased foil. Place the carrots in a large roasting tray and sit the beef on top of them. Place in the oven for 2½ hours, removing the foil for the final hour of cooking time.

When cooked, take the beef from the oven and leave it to rest for 20 minutes while you make gravy and cook the Yorkshire puddings.

Beat the eggs with the milk and the salt. Sieve the flour twice to aerate it and then beat the flour into the milk and egg mixture to make a batter. For extra smoothness, strain the batter. Place the Yorkshire tray in the oven until hot. Add a good amount of dripping into each pudding mould. Return the tray to the oven and heat until the fat is smoking. The fat will now be very hot, so take great care as you take the tray out of the oven. Ladle some of the batter into each mould until nearly full. Return the tray to the oven, reduce the heat to 200°C/400°F/Gas 6 and cook for 15 minutes.

Carve the rested beef and serve with the Yorkshire puddings, carrots and home-made gravy.

BEEF *and* PRUNE TAGINE

Serves 4–6

3 tbsp oil
600g chuck steak
1 tsp each cumin and coriander seeds, ground
1 tsp ground ginger
2 cloves, ground
¼ cinnamon stick, ground
pinch of saffron
salt and pepper
1 onion, grated
zest of ½ orange
1 tbsp honey
250g pitted prunes
100g almonds
1 tbsp chopped fresh coriander leaves, to serve

Preheat the oven to 150°C/300°F/Gas 2. In a large flameproof casserole or heavy-bottomed ovenproof saucepan, heat the oil and brown the beef well on all sides. Add the spices, salt and pepper and cook for a minute. Then add the grated onion and fry everything together for a further couple of minutes. Finally add the orange zest, honey and prunes and cover with cold water. Allow to come to the boil, add the almonds and stir well.

Cover the pan with a piece of baking parchment and the lid before putting it into the oven. Cook for 2½ hours; check occasionally and top up the water if necessary.

To serve, spoon into bowls and scatter with chopped coriander.

SKIRT STEAK
with MUSHROOMS *and* TARRAGON

Serves 2

2 x 200g skirt steaks
sea salt and black pepper
40g butter
4 shallots, diced
200g mushrooms, sliced
100ml white wine
1 tbsp chopped tarragon
1 tsp Dijon mustard, plus extra to serve

Season the steak well on both sides. In a hot frying pan, melt half of the butter and add the steak. After a few minutes, when browned well on one side, turn it over and cook for a few minutes on the other side. Turn the steak like this three or four times while cooking. The length of cooking time will depend on both the thickness of the steak and how well done you would like it. When cooked to your liking, remove the steak to a warm plate and allow to rest while you cook the mushrooms.

Pour any excess butter from the frying pan and wipe clean with a piece of kitchen towel. Return the pan to the heat and add the other half of the butter. Add the shallots and a little salt and cook gently for a few minutes until soft and sweet. Add the mushrooms, season well with salt and pepper and fry for several minutes until the mushrooms soften.

Pour in the wine and simmer to reduce by almost half. Add the tarragon and mustard and stir together to make a juicy mixture.

Place the steak on a wooden board and cut into thick slices. Serve with the mushrooms and extra Dijon mustard.

SUMMER BRAISED OXTAIL

Serves 4

2 tbsp plain flour
sea salt and pepper
4 pieces of oxtail, total weight around 800g
olive oil, for frying
300g carrots, cut into chunks
2 red onions, finely sliced
4 celery sticks, finely sliced
4 garlic cloves, finely sliced
1 tbsp each of chopped marjoram and parsley
200ml white wine
400g tin of plum tomatoes
1 bay leaf

Gremolata
1 bunch of parsley, finely chopped
zest of 1 lemon
1 garlic clove, finely chopped

Preheat the oven to 180°C/350°F/Gas 4. Put the flour on a plate and season well. Roll the pieces of oxtail in the flour and dust off any excess.

Heat the oil in a large flameproof casserole or heavy-bottomed ovenproof pan and brown the oxtail pieces on all sides. Remove from the pan and set aside.

Pour off any excess oil from the pan and wipe clean with kitchen towel. Add some more oil and gently fry the carrots, onion and celery with a little salt, until soft, but not brown. Stir in the garlic and chopped herbs and cook together for a few minutes before pouring in the wine. Let the wine reduce by half before adding the tomatoes and bay leaf. Return the oxtail to the pan.

Cover with a piece of baking parchment and the lid and place in the oven. Check after an hour and turn the pieces of oxtail over. Cook for at least 3 hours until the meat is tender.

For the gremolata, mix the parsley, lemon zest and garlic together in a bowl and chop through with a knife to blend the flavours.

To serve, spoon the braised oxtail into bowls and serve with the gremolata sprinkled on top.

GARLIC
with RECIPES *by*
CLARISSA DICKSON WRIGHT

Garlic is an indispensable ingredient in cooking, yet despite all its versatility, we only ever use one variety. To bring even more flavour to our cooking, we need to try one of our three fabulous native species of garlic or one of the cultivated varieties that are now being grown on British soil. When you start tasting these British-grown varieties you will find the flavours are as varied and complex as good wine or cheese.

Be surprised by the versatility of this little plant, use it raw in salsas and salads or slowly roast to an unctuous sweetness with thyme. Try a punchy aïoli with a platter of vegetables or summer-ripe tomatoes stuffed with delicious garlicky prawns and for something really unusual – a garlic fudge tart.

Garlic has fantastic medicinal attributes that have been used for centuries to cure all manner of ills. It is rich in vitamins A, B and C and its health-giving properties assist in lowering the risk of heart disease, ease indigestion and have wonderful antiseptic qualities. We now import 99% of our garlic from countries as far away as Mexico and China but compared to British-grown garlic, imported garlic not only has less flavour, but is also lower in allicin which contains garlic's natural nutrients.

Wild garlic grows abundantly all over the woods in spring, so you can even forage for your own or buy the leaves from local farmers' markets to make soups, risottos, or wild garlic pesto. Cultivated varieties are easy to grow in a pot or a small space in the garden, so you can harvest it fresh yourself.

It's time to think about this wonderful plant in a new way. Experiment with the varieties that flourish in Britain and experience a range of garlic flavour you may never have known.

BEEFSTEAK TOMATO
STUFFED *with* GARLIC PRAWNS

Garlic and tomatoes go well together and this dish is either a good starter to a meal or indeed an excellent supper dish. Elephant garlic has a mild nutty flavour. You want to use tomatoes that are ripe but not too soft. Cut your prawns into a size that will go comfortably into the tomato. If you have an oven that has a grill within it in the French style, you can finish the dish by browning the top. Put the dish in the middle of the oven and watch that it doesn't catch at the end. Alternatively finish it under your normal grill for a few minutes.
Clarissa Dickson Wright

Serves 4
- 4 beefsteak tomatoes, cut in half horizontally, seeds scooped out
- olive oil
- 1 elephant garlic clove, finely chopped
- 9 king prawns, cut into small pieces
- 6 tbsp white breadcrumbs
- 3 tbsp chopped parsley
- salt and pepper
- butter

Preheat the oven to 220°C/425°F/Gas 7. Place the halved tomatoes in an ovenproof dish. In a frying pan heat some oil. Fry the garlic and prawns gently in the oil. Mix in the breadcrumbs and parsley and season.

Stuff the tomatoes with the prawn and garlic mixture, dot with a little butter and bake in the oven for 20–25 minutes.

MEDIEVAL CHICKEN
with WHOLE GARLIC BULBS

When I said that I wanted to focus on garlic for this programme, the BBC's response was that garlic wasn't British. I pointed out that the word is of Anglo-Saxon origin and meant spear-leek. The Romans introduced garlic to Britain and now other types grow here very successfully as illustrated by Colin Boswell's work on The Garlic Farm on the Isle of Wight. As part of my persuasion, I promised that one of my recipes would be medieval and this dish is taken from *The Forme of Cury* (cury means cookery) a book compiled by the cooks to the Court of King Richard II in the late fourteenth century. Saffron was popular in the Middle Ages, a time when colour in food was a culinary obsession. You can roast all garlic bulbs whole, though elephant garlic is best wrapped in foil and when you come to eat them you squeeze the cloves and delicious paste oozes out. *Clarissa Dickson Wright*

Serves 4   small packet saffron threads
400ml white wine
1 roasting chicken
1 tsp each pepper and cinnamon
5 smallish bulbs of garlic
5cm piece of root ginger, finely chopped
olive oil
salt

Preheat the oven to 230°C/450°F/Gas 8. Soak the saffron in a little wine to soften. Rub the chicken all over with the pepper and cinnamon and place the chicken in an ovenproof dish. Cut the tops off the garlic bulbs until you can see the cloves and arrange the bulbs and chopped ginger around the chicken. Pour the oil into the garlic bulbs and pour the saffron and wine around the chicken. Season the chicken with salt and then place in the oven.

Roast for 20 minutes, then lower the oven temperature to 170°C/325°F/Gas 3 and cook for another 40 minutes, or until the juices run clear and the chicken is cooked. Regularly baste whilst cooking, paying special attention to basting the garlic.

GARLIC FUDGE TART
with NECTARINES

I am always one for a challenge and when my series producer asked for a pudding with garlic, my brain worked overtime. On the Garlic Farm, they sell garlic fudge (as well as garlic chocolate and garlic ice cream) and so using that I made this pudding. Lest you cannot buy garlic fudge, I have offered you this alternative. I can see you pulling a wry face but I do urge you to try the dish before you reject it out of hand. It will make a great talking point at your dinner table with your guests trying to work out the mystery ingredient. The nectarines were a fortuitous accident – I had just tried the garlic fudge and grabbed a nectarine to ameliorate the taste and thought 'Ahh!'. Choose fruit that are not too ripe and juicy. I dare you to go on and give it a go! *Clarissa Dickson Wright*

Serves 6

Pastry	*Filling*
150g plain flour	150g plain fudge
50g ground almonds	1 large garlic clove, mashed
25g caster sugar	100g Cheshire cheese, grated
85g unsalted butter,	3 large whole free range eggs
cut into small pieces	100ml double cream
1 free range egg, beaten	3 nectarines, stoned and halved

You will need a 23cm tart tin.

To make the pastry, put the flour, almonds, sugar and butter in a food processor and blitz until it resembles breadcrumbs, then slowly add the beaten egg. Or if you prefer you can make the whole thing by hand as I do. Bring the dough together, wrap in clingfilm and chill for at least an hour.

Once the pastry has rested, unwrap it and place on a lightly floured surface, roll out and use to line the tart tin. Prick the pastry all over with a fork and refrigerate for 2 hours or freeze for 30 minutes.

Meanwhile preheat the oven to 200°C/400°F/Gas 6. Bake blind for 15–20 minutes. Remove and leave to cool for about 10 minutes. Reduce the oven temperature to 160°C/312°F/Gas 2½.

In a food processor use the grating disc to cut up the fudge. Replace with the mixing blade and add all the other ingredients except the nectarines. Blend well.

Score the nectarines with three light cuts horizontally and vertically and place in the blind baked pastry case skin-side up. Pour in the filling. Bake in the centre of the oven for 20 minutes or until just set. Remove from the oven and leave to stand for a further 30 minutes.

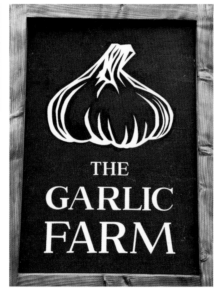

THE
GARLIC
FARM

AÏOLI PROVENÇALE

Serves 4–6   *Aïoli*
2 garlic cloves (4 if very fresh garlic), peeled
sea salt
3 very fresh, free range egg yolks
200ml olive oil
few squeezes of lemon juice

Vegetables
6 potatoes, peeled
6 carrots, peeled and halved
2 heads of fennel, cut into eighths
1 handful of green beans, topped and tailed
½ head cauliflower, broken into florets
1 handful of chopped parsley, to serve

To make the aïoli, crush the garlic cloves in a pestle and mortar with a little salt. Put the garlic into a bowl with the egg yolks and another pinch of salt. Using a whisk, add the olive oil, drop by drop at first, mixing all the time until the mixture starts to thicken. When the mixture thickens you can pour in the olive oil in a steady stream. When you have added all the oil, or if the aïoli has become too thick, add some lemon juice and mix well.

Put the potatoes into a large pan of cold, salted water and bring to the boil, then cook until tender. Drain and cool before slicing into wedges.

In another large pan of well salted, boiling water, cook the carrots until tender, remove and drain, then follow with the other vegetables, each variety at a time, topping up the water as necessary.

When all the vegetables are cooked and drained, arrange on a large serving platter and sprinkle with chopped parsley.

To serve, spoon the aïoli into a bowl and place in the middle of the platter, for everyone to help themselves.

SPATCHCOCK CHICKEN MARINATED
in YOGURT *and* WILD GARLIC

Serves 4

4 cardamom pods
pinch of saffron
1 tsp cumin seeds
1 tsp ground turmeric
2 large handfuls of wild garlic leaves, washed
100ml yogurt
salt and pepper
1 spatchcock chicken (ask your butcher to do this for you)
olive oil

Crush the cardamom pods to release the tiny black seeds inside. Discard the green husky outer layer. In a hot, dry frying pan, lightly toast the saffron and the cumin seeds. Tip them into a pestle and mortar and crush with the cardamom seeds. Add the ground turmeric to the crushed spices and mix well.

In a food processor, or carefully by hand, finely chop the garlic leaves. Remove to a bowl, add the spices and yogurt and mix well. Season well with salt and pepper. Smear the marinade evenly over the bird, covering both sides. Cover and leave to marinate in the fridge for at least an hour.

To cook, preheat the grill. Place the marinated bird on a grill pan and pour over a little olive oil. Cook for 10 minutes, skin-side down. Carefully turn the bird over and cook, skin-side up, for a further 5 minutes or so; watch carefully to make sure it does not burn (as it tends to with the yogurt marinade).

Slice the chicken and serve with rice, vegetables and extra yogurt and garlic leaves if required.

TURKEY
with RECIPES *by* ANGELA HARTNETT

These wonderful big birds have been in our country for centuries. Tender, succulent and very healthy (they are low in fat and rich in protein), turkey can be cooked in so many delicious ways; baked in a pie, spicy in a curry or braised to tenderness with wine and herbs. It is time to remember how to cook with this beautiful fowl.

It is thought that turkeys came to Britain during our trade years with the Levant or merchants from Turkey, hence their name. They were so gastronomically valuable that in 1541 they were placed under 'sumptuary law', a law which regulated the public's habits of consumption. By 1557 we were eating them for our Christmas dinners, after they had 'been fattened with rounceval peas'. The Elizabethans cooked them in pies or roasted them with claret, orange juice and lemon peel. Later, Elizabeth David talks of them 'spit roasted with sausage and potato and served with dandelion and beetroot salad'.

White breeds of turkey started appearing on our Christmas lunch tables in the 1960s. Before that date, our seasonal centrepiece would have been a bronze turkey. Fortunately some breeders kept up the older traditions and breeds. Bronze turkeys are raised slowly and allowed to hang for 14 days. Some turkeys like, the Norfolk black, have also been recognised as native rare breeds but it's about us enjoying them on more occasions than one day a year which will ensure their survival.

Because of the size of these birds, there are often leftovers which can be transformed into delicious dishes like a Turkish-inspired spiced pilaf or in a rich devilled sauce, turkey tonnato or turkey curry.

Ask your butcher for these fantastic bronze turkeys, find them in farmers' markets or buy direct from a supplier. The turkey season runs from November to May, so it's time to revive the fortunes of this delicious and versatile meat and enjoy cooking and eating it on many more days and in many more ways.

TURKEY CURRY

I'm not a big coconut or coriander fan, but this recipe uses both of these ingredients and it's one dish when I enjoy eating them. Along with the turkey, it makes a delicious, healthy curry. And if you really want to make it super-slimming, remove the potatoes from the recipe.
Angela Hartnett

Serves 4

1 onion, chopped

4 fresh birdseye chillies, deseeded and chopped

1 tsp coriander seeds

2 tsp tamarind paste

1 tbsp caster sugar

2 garlic cloves, bruised

1 small knob of root ginger, peeled and chopped

1 tbsp sunflower oil, for frying

500g turkey breast, sliced

3 sprigs of thyme, leaves only

400ml coconut milk

150ml chicken or turkey stock

2 large waxy potatoes, peeled and diced

250g fresh spinach, chopped

1 bunch of fresh coriander, chopped

50g whole peeled almonds

Put the chopped onion, chillies, coriander seeds, tamarind, sugar, one clove of garlic and ginger into a blender or food processor and blitz until blended into a paste.

In a large frying pan, heat the oil and add the turkey (in two batches if needed), other garlic clove and thyme and sauté for a few minutes to brown the turkey. Remove from the pan and discard the garlic. In the same pan, add the blended paste and lightly roast for a few minutes. Remove from the pan. Return the turkey to the pan, cover with the coconut milk and stock and add the potatoes.

Leave to cook for 20 minutes until the turkey has cooked and the sauce thickened. Finally, stir in the spinach, coriander and almonds and allow to warm through. Remove from the heat and serve.

TURKEY, LEEK *and* HAM PIE

There are certain marriages that work in cooking, and tarragon, cream and white meat such as turkey is a perfect combination. Add some leek, ham and a lid of puff pastry and you've got a delicious supper dish. It's a one-pot wonder that can be prepared in advance and a great way of adding hidden vegetables to give to your children. *Angela Hartnett*

Serves 4

butter, for frying
1 large onion, chopped
2 large carrots, sliced into lozenges
2 large leeks, sliced into 2cm pieces, washed well
200ml double cream
200ml chicken or turkey stock
500g cooked turkey, cut into bite-sized pieces
200g cooked ham, cut into bite-sized pieces
10 button mushrooms, halved
pinch of cayenne pepper
2 tbsp chopped tarragon
thyme leaves
salt and fresh black pepper
225g frozen puff pastry, defrosted
1 free range egg, beaten, for glazing
2 tbsp Parmesan, finely grated

You will need a 1-pint ceramic pie dish.

Preheat the oven to 200°C/400°F/Gas 6. Heat a large pan over a medium heat. Add a knob of butter and sauté the onion until soft but not coloured. Add the carrots and leek and sauté for 5 minute until the carrots start to become soft. Cover with the cream and stock and simmer until it starts to thicken. Finish by adding the turkey, ham, mushrooms, cayenne and herbs. Season and adjust to taste.

Take off the heat and pour the filling into a ceramic pie dish. Roll out enough pastry to cover the dish and cut an additional strip to edge the rim of the pie dish. Press down firmly and seal all around. Brush with beaten egg and sprinkle with Parmesan. Cook in the oven for 20 minutes until the pastry is golden.

TURKEY BRAISED IN RED WINE

This is my take on a classic French coq au vin. It's a great way to use the darker meat of the turkey. I love to add more vegetables than the classic dish because then it finishes it as a complete dish. And remember to use good-quality red wine – you really will savour the difference. *Angela Hartnett*

Serves 6

2 turkey legs, cut into thighs
   and drumsticks
2 turkey wings

Marinade
1 bottle of good-quality red wine
   (Pinot Noir or Burgundy)
2 small onions, roughly chopped
2 celery sticks, roughly chopped
2 medium carrots, roughly chopped
4 garlic cloves, roughly chopped
thyme leaves
black peppercorns

1 bay leaf

Casserole
butter, for frying
150g pancetta, cut into thick dice
15 button mushrooms
15 baby onions, peeled
100g plain flour, seasoned
1 carrot, sliced
1 celery stick, sliced
sprigs of thyme
1 bay leaf
flat-leaf parsley, chopped

Place all of the marinade ingredients in a bowl, add the turkey pieces and leave to marinate preferably overnight or for at least 6 hours.

When you are ready to braise the turkey, heat a large pan or flameproof casserole dish and melt a knob of butter in the pan. Add the pancetta and lightly brown. Remove from the pan. In the same pan, cook the mushrooms and onions for a few minutes until they colour and then remove from the pan. Place the pan to one side.

Remove the turkey from the marinade and strain the liquid over a bowl. Discard the vegetables but reserve the wine.

Gently dip the turkey into the seasoned flour. Return the large pan to the hob on a high heat and brown the coated turkey pieces on all sides.

Turn down the heat and add the mushrooms, onions, carrot and celery along with the thyme and bay leaf. Pour in the reserved wine and simmer for 1 hour. When ready, allow to rest and then add the parsley.

TURKEY TONNATO

Serves 4

400g cooked turkey fillet, finely sliced
1 free range egg yolk
100ml olive oil
100g canned tuna, broken into pieces
4 anchovy fillets, finely chopped
juice of ½ lemon
sea salt and pepper
2 tbsp capers
1 handful of rocket leaves
lemon wedges, to serve

Lay the slices of turkey on a plate. Put the egg yolk in a bowl and add the oil, drop by drop, whisking all the time. When it starts to emulsify, pour in the rest of the oil in a steady stream. Add the tuna pieces, anchovy and lemon juice and season well. Mix together to make a thick sauce.

Spread the sauce over the turkey and sprinkle with the capers and rocket leaves. Season with salt and pepper and serve with lemon wedges.

TURKEY SALTIMBOCCA

Serves 2
200g cooked turkey breast, thinly sliced into 6 long strips
2 large slices of ham
12 sage leaves
20g butter
salt and pepper
100ml white wine

You will need two sheets of greaseproof paper and six wooden cocktail sticks.

Preheat the oven to 220°C/425°F/Gas 7. Lay a turkey strip on a sheet of greaseproof paper. Cover with the other sheet of paper and, using a rolling pin, lightly tap or roll over the top sheet of paper to flatten and stretch the turkey to about 2mm thick. Repeat with the other five pieces.

Lay the turkey slices on a board. Slice the ham into six pieces, each the same size as the turkey slices. Place a piece of ham onto each turkey slice and two sage leaves on top of the ham. Roll up the pieces and secure with a cocktail stick.

In a frying pan, melt the butter and add the little rolled parcels. Season well and fry to brown on all sides. When they are browned all over, add the wine and let it bubble to reduce by almost half.

Put the little rolls and the wine into a baking dish and bake in the oven for 10 minutes. When cooked, place all of the parcels on a plate and pour over the wine sauce. Serve with a simple green salad.

MACKEREL
with RECIPES *by* RICHARD CORRIGAN

Mackerel have smooth greeny-blue skin, marked with black streaks and a silver belly, which makes them one of the most striking looking fish. These beautiful fish are abundant in our sea, what needs reviving is our taste for them. Grilled, fried, pickled and smoked, the mackerel is the prince of fish – enjoyed all over the world – but not enough in Britain.

Mackerel is high in health-giving oils and its firm, white flesh has a rich flavour. Fresh mackerel tastes excellent grilled or fried with a sauce of tart fruits such as gooseberry or rhubarb or try it with a chutney of greengages. The Spanish like to grill mackerel with garlic and paprika, both strong flavours which this fish can stand up to.

It is perfect to smoke, remaining succulent because of its natural oils. Serve with lots of pepper, lemon or a sorrel salad, or make it into a delicious pâté with chopped cornichons and horseradish. Try buying fresh mackerel and then home-smoking it with the recipe for tea-smoked mackerel with crab apple jelly on page 157.

Ninety per cent of our mackerel gets exported, mainly to Russia, Japan, the Far East, Africa and France. The Japanese slice it into sashimi and eat it raw. Many countries and cuisines all appreciate and use this lovely fish; it's time for us to do the same.

Look for fish with bright eyes and firm flesh. A single mackerel is usually the perfect portion size, which makes judging quantities easy. You will also find they are one of the less expensive fish on the fishmonger's slab. It's plentiful, it's healthy, it tastes good; it's time to keep some to enjoy for ourselves.

MACKEREL *and* SQUID ROLL

Inspired by a burger once eaten in a Soho restaurant where they combined both mackerel and squid. Both of these are in abundance and readily available. Often a spring roll is a disappointment but this is an explosion of tastes and textures. *Richard Corrigan*

Serves 5

Rolls

1 onion, finely sliced
2 carrots, finely sliced
2 spring onions, finely sliced
2 celery stalks, finely sliced
2 green chillies, finely sliced
250g squid, cleaned and finely sliced
4 fillets of mackerel, chopped
   into small pieces
1 tbsp fish sauce
50g roast peanuts, chopped
juice of 1 lime
1 small knob of root ginger,
   peeled and grated

1 tsp sesame seeds
20g plain flour
100ml warm water
10 sheets of spring roll pastry
vegetable oil, for frying

Dipping sauce

juice of 4 limes
20g sugar
25ml soy sauce
50ml rice wine vinegar
50ml mirin

In a hot pan or wok, flash fry all the vegetables, remove from the pan. Put the squid and mackerel in the pan and cook for 30 seconds, then remove.

In a bowl, mix the hot fish and vegetables with the fish sauce, roasted peanuts, juice of one lime, ginger and sesame seeds and cool.

Mix the flour into the warm water and stir to make into a thin paste. Lay out the pastry sheets and brush each sheet all over with the paste. Divide the filling mix into five and wrap with one sheet of the pastry. Then wrap each roll with a second sheet to ensure crispiness. Heat the oil to 180°C/350°F in a deep-fat fryer or large saucepan. Fry the rolls until golden brown and crisp.

To make the dipping sauce, mix the juice of the four limes, the sugar, soy sauce, vinegar and mirin together in a bowl.

Serve the rolls immediately while hot, alongside the dipping sauce.

MACKEREL
with WARM GREENGAGE CHUTNEY

This is a British recipe which goes back to Victorian times and making the delicious greengage chutney will brighten up any typical British wintery day. Oily fish leaves a slight aftertaste so introducing the sweet and sour flavour of greengage neutralises the acid in the mackerel. *Richard Corrigan*

Serves 4

Chutney
olive oil
1 onion, finely chopped
2 garlic cloves, finely chopped
1 tsp mustard seeds
1 tsp ground ginger
½ tsp ground turmeric
½ tsp ground cardamom
2 star anise

4 tomatoes, peeled, deseeded
   and chopped
100ml white wine vinegar
50g sugar
salt
12 greengages, roughly chopped

Mackerel
4 mackerel fillets
vegetable oil, for frying

To make the chutney, heat the olive oil in a large pan and cook the onion and garlic until soft. Add the mustard seeds, ground ginger, turmeric, cardamom, star anise and stir. Add the tomatoes, vinegar, sugar and salt and simmer until everything thickens. Once thick, add the greengages and cook until soft. Remove from the heat and allow to cool slightly.

To fry the mackerel, heat the oil in a large, heavy frying pan. Place each mackerel fillet skin-side down and fry for about 5 minutes to cook though. Serve the mackerel with spoonfuls of the warm greengage chutney.

TEA-SMOKED MACKEREL
with CRAB APPLE JELLY

Mackerel has to be served fresh but tea-smoking preserves it and introduces a very delicate flavor. The mackerel can be smoked over a stove indoors or outside, great for a barbeque. Crab apple jelly is sweet and sour and it's a great way of using free food, so this is a very cheap recipe to make. *Richard Corrigan*

Serves 4

Crab apple jelly
500g crab apples, peeled and halved
250g sugar
water, to cover
gelatine leaves, soaked

Tea-smoked mackerel
100g white rice
100g demerara sugar
25g tea leaves of your choice
   i.e. jasmine, camomile
8 mackerel fillets
salt and pepper
oil, for greasing

Put the apples and sugar in a pan and pour in enough water to cover. Bring to the boil and cook until the apples are soft and falling apart.

Strain the cooked apples through a sieve and pour the strained liquid into a measuring jug. For every 500ml of liquid, you will need two leaves of the softened gelatine. Add the gelatine to the liquid while it is still hot, stir to dissolve, strain again and then chill the jelly in the fridge.

To make the smoking mixture, put the rice, demerara sugar and tea leaves into a bowl and mix together. Line a deep pan or a wok with foil, place over a high heat and tip in the smoking mixture.

Season the mackerel. Rub a cooling rack with a little oil and place the mackerel on the rack, skin-side down. When the mixture begins to smoke, place the rack on top of the pan or wok and cover with foil. Turn off the heat and let the mackerel cook slowly as it cools.

When cooked, place the tea-smoked mackerel fillets on each plate and serve with the crab apple jelly.

SMOKED MACKEREL
and CORNICHON PÂTÉ

Serves 4   250g smoked mackerel fillets
100ml crème fraîche
2 tsp grated horseradish
cayenne pepper
1 tbsp cornichons, chopped finely
lemon juice, to taste
salt and freshly ground black pepper

Remove the skin from the mackerel and, using your fingers, break the flesh into small pieces. Place in a bowl with the crème fraîche, horseradish and cayenne and, using a fork, beat the mixture together to make a rough pâté.

Stir in the cornichons and season with the lemon juice, pepper and a little salt.

Serve with hot toast and butter.

MACKEREL
with GOOSEBERRY SAUCE

Serves 2   20g butter
             250g gooseberries, topped and tailed
             2 tsp sugar
             pinch of cayenne pepper
             sea salt and pepper
             4 mackerel fillets
             oil, for frying

Melt the butter in a saucepan and add the gooseberries, sugar, cayenne and a little salt and pepper. Cook gently for about 5 minutes until the gooseberries are soft and starting to collapse into a thick sauce. Check for seasoning and adjust as necessary. Pass the mixture through a sieve and spoon the sauce into a pan. Place on a low heat to keep warm.

Season the mackerel fillets well and heat the oil in a frying pan. When it is hot, add the mackerel fillets, skin-side down and cook until the colour of the flesh starts to turn white, Turn over and cook for another minute flesh-side down.

To serve, lay two fillets on each plate and spoon over the gooseberry sauce. Serve with potatoes and a sweet vegetable such as peas to complement the tartness of the sauce.

CURRANTS
with RECIPES *by* MATT TEBBUTT

These beautiful little red, white or dark purple jewel-like fruits that hang in bright clusters were once a common feature of British cooking. They were used in jellies, jams and traditional puddings, championed by the ever-popular Eliza Acton, whose seminal book on family cooking was published in 1845.

Black, red and white – all colours are crucial in summer pudding but the differing fruit and colours also come into their own in solo starring roles. Redcurrants have a great use in savoury dishes; classic Cumberland sauce which Elizabeth David referred to as 'this best of all sauces for cold meat' or redcurrant jelly with lamb. Blackcurrants are very versatile, working well with the dark, rich meat of wild duck or equally delicious made into sorbet or ice cream as well as baked in custard-filled tarts. Whitecurrant is a mild and sweeter variety of redcurrant which works well in creamy, velvety desserts.

The British blackcurrant is of a very high quality as they are bred for their deep colour, which is packed with health-promoting antioxidants and is very high in vitamin C. The Glaswegian author Nancy Brysson Morrison in her novel of 1949, *The Winnowing Years*, writes of 'black-currant tea for a sore throat, and dumpsy-dearie when the children were good'. Over 95% of British blackcurrants are sold to make Ribena (currants are from the Ribes family, hence the name) and whilst this provides a steady income for growers it does mean this most British of fruits is disappearing from British cooking.

Let us learn to love this forgotten fruit again. Throughout the summer, currants can be used fresh in puddings, salads and meat dishes. Then, to appreciate them for the rest of the year, bottle as cordials, preserve as jams or jellies and enjoy them beyond their season.

WILD DUCK
with BLACKCURRANT
and CASSIS SAUCE

Wild duck sits very comfortably alongside these delicious blackcurrants. They have a natural affinity; the tartness of the berry work so well with the dark richness of the duck. The cassis adds an extra dimension to the finished sauce, a deep fruitiness that only these darkly-glinting berries can bring. *Matt Tebbutt*

Serves 2

1 wild duck
1 square of pork back fat
salt and pepper

Blackcurrant and cassis sauce
50g butter
3 shallots, finely diced
sprig of thyme
splash of red wine vinegar
150ml red port
150ml red wine
50ml cassis
50ml blackcurrant juice
1 tbsp blackcurrants

Preheat the oven to 180°C/350°F/Gas 4. Truss the duck and lay a square of pork back fat over the breast. Season well. Place the bird in a roasting tin and put in the oven. After 10 minutes of cooking time, remove the pork fat to allow the breast to brown. Cook for a further 40 minutes and while cooking baste the bird every so often. Remove from the oven and rest somewhere warm.

In a saucepan, melt half of the butter and sweat the shallots with the thyme sprig for 10 minutes. Add the vinegar and let it bubble for 30 seconds. Pour in the port, red wine and cassis. Reduce to almost a syrup and then add the blackcurrant juice and simmer for 5 minutes. Add the blackcurrants and warm gently. Finally whisk in the remaining butter and remove from the heat.

Carve the rested duck, arrange the slices on warmed plates and spoon the sauce around the duck slices. Serve with game chips and watercress.

GLAZED HAM
with REDCURRANT *and* CITRUS JELLY

Redcurrant jelly is a classic recipe of great British cookery. It is the perfect foil not only for this fatty meat, but it also works well with oily fish such as mackerel. It's a recipe I enjoy making at the end of the summer months, storing away little pots of the stuff, ready to bring out throughout the looming winter months ahead. *Matt Tebbutt*

Serves 6

1 cooked corner of ham

Redcurrant and citrus jelly
1kg redcurrants
preserving sugar
juice and zest of 3 oranges
juice and zest of 3 lemons
150ml red port
50ml red wine vinegar
2 cloves

1 cinnamon stick
pinch of ground ginger

Glaze
150g runny honey
100g demerara sugar
sprigs of fresh thyme
50ml redcurrant juice
25ml red wine vinegar
½ tsp English mustard

Put the redcurrants into a pan with a little water, bring to a simmer and allow the fruit to burst. Tip into a jelly bag and strain overnight into a large bowl.

Next day, measure the liquid, place in a pan and add 450g of preserving sugar to every 600ml of juice created. Dissolve over a rapid heat and boil for 5–10 minutes. Set aside the redcurrant jelly until required.

Preheat the oven to 190°C/375°F/Gas 5. In a saucepan boil the orange and lemon juice with the zest. Reduce the heat, and add the port, vinegar and spices. Simmer for 20 minutes and then add 300g of the prepared redcurrant jelly and simmer for a further 10 minutes. Remove from the heat and allow to cool.

Place all the glaze ingredients in a pan over a low heat until the honey and sugar dissolve. Remove from the heat and allow to cool.

Slash the surface of the ham in a diamond pattern and rub in the glaze. Place in a roasting tin and put into the oven for 40–50 minutes. Continue to baste the ham with the glaze while it heats in the oven.

When glazed, allow the ham to cool to room temperature and then slice. Serve with the redcurrant and citrus jelly, and a celery, apple and fresh parsley salad and chunks of bread.

WHITECURRANT *and* WHISKY SEMIFREDDO

The cordial in this recipe is so packed full of whitecurrant goodness it could almost be considered medicinal. Serve over ice with a little water; it makes a delicious drink in itself, and with a rather good whisky hit to boot. By adding it to the base of this soft-setting cream, it becomes elevated to a wonderfully rich and velvety dessert. *Matt Tebbutt*

Serves 6

Whisky cordial
150ml whisky
75g whitecurrants
40g sugar
zest of ½ lemon
½ tsp peeled and grated
   root ginger

Semifreddo
4 free range egg yolks
50–75g caster sugar
250ml double cream

To scatter
extra whitecurrants, macerated

You will need six 125ml pudding moulds, lined with clingfilm.

To make the whisky cordial, place the whisky, whitecurrants, sugar, zest and ginger in a saucepan over a low heat. Mix the ingredients together and allow to infuse. Do not allow to boil. Strain and push the pulp through a sieve to extract the juice. Set aside.

Place the egg yolks and sugar in a bowl over simmering water and whisk until thick. Take the pan off the heat and continue to whisk until cool.

Add 125ml of the whisky cordial to the egg mixture, a tablespoon at a time until fully incorporated. Whisk the double cream to thick ribbons and fold into the mixture. Pour into the lined moulds and freeze overnight.

Take the extra whitecurrants and prick all over with a pin. Place in a bowl with the remaining whisky cordial and macerate overnight.

To serve, remove the semifreddo from the moulds onto plates and scatter with the macerated currants.

SPARKLING RED *and* WHITECURRANT JELLY

Serves 4   400g mixed red and whitecurrants, plus 50g to finish, stalks removed
150g caster sugar
zest and juice of ½ lemon
zest and juice of ½ orange
12 gelatine leaves, (fine leaf, prepare according to the packet instructions)
500ml sparkling wine, very chilled

You will need a 1-litre jelly mould, lightly greased with a light oil, groundnut is good.

Put 400g of the currants in a saucepan with the sugar, zest and juice. Simmer gently for about 5 minutes until the currants soften and start to break apart.

Using a jelly bag or sieve lined with double thickness muslin, strain the juice from the currants into a bowl.

To prepare the gelatine, soak it in blood-temperature water for about 10 minutes to soften.

In a pan, very gently warm the juice from the currants, do not allow to boil. Remove the softened gelatine from the water and add to the juice. Stir well to dissolve. Pour the syrup into a shallow container and put in the fridge to cool.

When the mixture is very cool and beginning to thicken (after about 30 minutes), add the sparkling wine, pouring very slowly to prevent it from bubbling over.

Put the remaining 50g of currants into the bottom of the mould, and then pour in the rest of the jelly mixture. Cover and chill in the fridge for at least 4 hours or until it is set but still has a little wobble.

You can make this the day before but the longer you leave it to chill, the more set the jelly becomes.

CUMBERLAND SAUCE

Serves 6–8
2 oranges
1 lemon
225g redcurrant jelly
2 tsp Dijon mustard
5 tbsp port
1 tsp cornflour
salt and pepper

Pare the zest from the oranges and the lemon. Mix the zests together and divide into two equal amounts. Juice the zested fruit and set aside the juice.

Bring a small saucepan of water to the boil and blanch one half of the zest for a minute. Remove and drain. When cooled, finely shred with a knife.

Meanwhile, finely shred the unblanched zest and put into a saucepan with the redcurrant jelly, mustard, and orange and lemon juice.

In a separate pan, heat the port to a boil. Boil for a minute to burn off the alcohol before adding to the jelly mixture.

Finally, mix the cornflour with a little water to make a paste and add to the jelly mixture with the salt and pepper. Heat the pan with the jelly mixture over a gentle heat for 5 minutes, stirring constantly. Remove from the heat and strain through a sieve. Add the remaining blanched zest and allow to cool.

It can be eaten hot or cold with cold meats. Poured into a jar, it can be stored in the fridge for a couple of weeks.

EGGS

with RECIPES *by* JAMES MARTIN

Eggs are used in virtually every type of cooking, almost everywhere in the world, and have been throughout history. The Classical Greeks boiled them, the Romans turned them into custards and in the Middle Ages they roasted them in embers.

Eggs are among the most nutritient-dense food available to us. They are a rich source of vitamins A, D, B, iron and folic acid as well as antioxidants.

Between us, we eat over a whopping 11 million hens' eggs a year in the UK. But what about the other types of eggs we could be eating? In the past, we used to enjoy eggs from duck, geese and quail.

Before World War II, duck eggs were widely used and enjoyed. Larger than hens' eggs, they are a great source of protein, have a delicious flavour and are excellent for use in baking. Farmers who are reviving their use have been working hard to ensure that their duck eggs are of the highest standard, both in animal welfare and the quality of eggs.

Wild quail used to appear in England in the summer, where they would feed in the cornfields. The birds and their eggs are small, but these naturally shy and timid creatures display a great sense of adventure. Now specialist quail farms exist to provide us with these little delicacies all year round. Quail eggs are wonderful simply boiled and dipped in salt or even cumin seeds. Or they can be poached or fried as bite-sized tapas.

Mrs Beeton extolled the virtues of different kinds of eggs and she was right. To ignore duck and quail eggs is to ignore our British heritage. This is our chance to start experimenting with new tastes. Look for hens' eggs that come from special varieties of birds, always choose free range and organic where possible, but don't stop there; try baking with duck eggs or putting tasty quail eggs into dishes.

ARBROATH SMOKIE PÂTÉ
with SOFT QUAIL EGGS *and* BEETROOT

Quails are funny birds, as I discovered while wandering around the quail farm in Sussex making the show. The little-man syndrome even extends to our feathered little friends…they make a lot of noise for such little things! The eggs are the opposite – small, yet delicate in flavour. Arbroath smokies too are a real delight, they also have a great flavour and this pâté takes just seconds to make in the blender. *James Martin*

Serves 4

Pâté
2 Arbroath smokies
juice of 2 lemons
150ml double cream
20g fresh chives, finely chopped
sea salt
freshly ground black pepper
butter, melted (optional)

Dressing
50ml sherry vinegar
50ml red wine vinegar
300ml extra virgin olive oil

Salad
mixed leaves; baby red chard,
    lamb's tongue, watercress,
    Little Gem
2 small quail eggs, soft-boiled
    and peeled
300g cooked beetroot, sliced
fresh chervil leaves, to garnish

Remove the flesh from the fish, discarding all the skin and bones, and place into a blender. Add the lemon juice, and with the blender mixing quickly, add the double cream. Whiz to a smooth but not too smooth pâté. Remove the pâté from the blender into a bowl, add the chives and season well.

Place into a pot and smooth over the surface. If keeping overnight, cover the surface of the pâté with a thin layer of melted butter to stop it discolouring and place in the fridge. When ready to use, shape the pâté into quenelles.

Make the dressing by placing both vinegars in a bowl. Whisk in 225ml of the olive oil, check the flavour for balance of oil and acidity and add more oil if needed. (If placed in a container, this oil with keep for a month; it is the one I use as the house dressing in our restaurants.)

Dress the salad leaves with a little of the vinaigrette and cut the eggs in half. Place the beetroot in overlapping circles on a plate, place the salad leaves on top of the beetroot, top with the pâté and the soft-boiled eggs, and garnish with a few chervil leaves. Serve with slices of warm Melba toast.

DEEP-FRIED CRISPY DUCK EGG
with DUCK CONFIT SALAD

At first this may appear difficult, but it's a simple matter of timing; once mastered, this will give you the perfect soft-boiled egg when peeled. We do it in the restaurant with a ham hock terrine and once the eggs are covered in the breadcrumbs, they can be stored in the fridge for 24 hours before use. Duck eggs are so good for this because they create a nice dressing from the soft egg yolk that goes brilliantly with the duck and bacon. *James Martin*

Serves 4

Crispy eggs
5 free range duck eggs
2 tbsp white wine vinegar
salt and freshly ground black pepper
110g plain flour
200g fresh breadcrumbs
vegetable oil, for deep-frying

Duck confit salad
120ml rice wine vinegar
2 tbsp sugar
2 large shallots, finely sliced

100g cherries, stoned
2 tbsp sherry vinegar
50ml extra virgin olive oil
50g frisée lettuce
coriander cress
10g pea shoots
1 ready-made confit duck leg,
    meat picked from bone and
    roughly chopped
salt and freshly ground black pepper
4 slices of streaky bacon, cooked until
    crisp between two baking sheets

For the crispy eggs, bring a large pot of water to the boil. Add the vinegar and a pinch of salt. Set a bowl of iced water alongside. Boil four of the eggs in the water for exactly 5 minutes, remove from the pan using a slotted spoon and chill in the iced water. Crack the remaining egg into a bowl. Whisk and add a pinch of salt and freshly ground black pepper. Sprinkle the flour and breadcrumbs into two separate shallow dishes and season with salt and freshly ground black pepper.

Peel the cooled boiled eggs. One at a time, gently dredge the eggs in the flour until evenly coated. Next, dip them in the whisked egg, then roll in the breadcrumbs until completely coated. Chill in the fridge.

Meanwhile, for the salad, place the rice wine vinegar, sugar and a pinch of salt into a pan and bring to the boil. Pour over the shallots and cherries and leave to cool.

For the dressing, pour the sherry vinegar and olive oil into a jug and whisk. Place the salad leaves into a bowl and flake in the pieces of duck confit. Strain off the shallots and cherries and add to the salad with the dressing and mix. Season to taste.

Just before serving, heat the vegetable oil in a deep-fat fryer to 180°C/350°F. Roll the chilled, coated eggs in more breadcrumbs, then deep-fry until golden brown. Remove from the oil using a slotted spoon and set aside to drain on kitchen paper. Sprinkle with salt.

Place the dressed salad onto the plates in a little nest and cut the crispy egg open at the top and place in the centre of the salad. Cut the bacon into small pieces, scatter around the egg and serve with a little more of the dressing poured around.

STRAWBERRIES *and* CREAM SPONGE CAKE

Forget the diet, this is proper cooking! It's quick too, as the jam really only takes a few minutes to cook. Making the sponge with duck eggs will not only give a richer colour and make it more yellow, but due to the fat content of the eggs, it will make a lighter cake that will last longer if making it in advance. A classic Victoria sponge it isn't. (That would be without cream and would use raspberry jam with a topping of caster sugar.) But trust me on this: it's one of the best cake recipes I have ever made. *James Martin*

Serves 4–6

Strawberry jam
500g strawberries, hulled and cut
  in half only if large
500g jam sugar
juice of ½ lemon

Sponge cake
250g butter, at room temperature,
  plus extra for greasing
250g caster sugar

pinch of salt
5 duck eggs
250g self-raising flour, plus extra
  for dusting
200ml double cream, softly whipped

To decorate
100g sugar
strawberries, stems left on
icing sugar, for dusting

You will need two x 20cm, and at least 4cm deep, loose-bottom sponge tins.

Tip the strawberries, sugar and lemon juice into a large pan and stir over a moderate heat for 2–3 minutes or until the sugar has dissolved. Turn up the heat and boil for 5 minutes, you don't have to check for a setting point as this is an instant jam. Remove from the heat, pour into a tray and set aside to cool. The jam will keep in the fridge for up to a week.

Preheat the oven to 190°C/375°F/Gas 5. Lightly grease and flour the tins and line the bases with parchment paper.

Beat the butter, sugar and a pinch of salt together until well creamed. Gently beat the eggs in a small bowl and then add them, a little at a time, to the creamed sugar and butter mixture.

When all the eggs have been incorporated, gently fold in the flour and divide the mixture equally between the two lined tins.

Bake for 25–30 minutes, until well risen and golden brown on top. Remove from the oven and turn out onto a wire cooling rack. Peel off the parchment paper and leave to cool completely.

Meanwhile, heat the sugar in a small pan over a moderate heat until it starts to turn a pale caramel colour. Remove from the heat and dip the strawberries into the caramel. Dry and cool on a non-stick mat.

Place one of the sponges on a plate or cake stand and spread with the cream and strawberry jam. Add the second sponge on top and dust with icing sugar. Finish by placing the caramel-dipped strawberries on top of the cake.

FONDUTA SAUCE
with ASPARAGUS *and* POACHED EGG

Serves 2
- ½ garlic clove
- 2 free range egg yolks
- 100g crème fraîche
- 50g Parmesan, grated
- sea salt and pepper
- 300g asparagus spears
- 2 free range eggs

Rub the inside of a heatproof bowl with the cut garlic. Add the egg yolks, crème fraîche and Parmesan to the bowl, season well and whisk together. Place the bowl over a pan of boiling water. Make sure the bowl doesn't touch the water. Continue to whisk, the mixture will be quite liquid to start with but as it heats and the yolks cook, it will begin to thicken. This will take up to 10 minutes, by which time the sauce should be the consistency of very thick cream.

Meanwhile, bring a large pan of water to the boil. Add a teaspoon of salt and cook the asparagus for a couple of minutes or until just soft. Remove with a slotted spoon and drain.

For the eggs, bring a pan of water to a simmer. Break each egg gently into the water. Poach for 3–4 minutes or until the white is firm but the yolk still soft. Remove with a slotted spoon and drain.

Lay the asparagus spears on a dish, place the eggs on top, and pour over the thick sauce. Season well and eat immediately. This makes an excellent lunch or light supper dish.

SPINACH, FETA *and* HERB FRITTATA

Serves 2   1 large bunch of spinach, stalks removed
20g butter
2 spring onions, sliced
1 handful of mixed herbs, roughly chopped (parsley, coriander, dill and mint)
50g feta, crumbled
few pinches of allspice
6 free range eggs
salt and pepper

Cook the spinach in salted water. When ready, drain and squeeze out any excess liquid and roughly chop.

Melt most of the butter in a pan and gently sweat the spring onions until they are soft. Put the spinach, onions, herbs, feta and allspice into a bowl. Break in the eggs and mix gently to keep strands of the white and yolk separate. Season well.

Preheat the grill. Heat a frying pan until hot and melt a little butter in it. Pour in the mixture and cook a little until the bottom of the frittata has set. Remove from the heat and place the pan under the grill for the top to cook.

Eat warm with a green salad.

RASPBERRY *and* PASSION FRUIT SOUFFLÉ

Serves 8

4 free range egg yolks
80g caster sugar
40g plain flour
10g cornflour
280ml milk
250g raspberries
3 passion fruit, pulp and seeds scooped out
butter, for greasing
icing sugar, sifted, for dusting
8 free range egg whites

You will need eight individual soufflé dishes.

Preheat the oven to 180°C/350°F/Gas 4. Place the egg yolks and sugar in a bowl and beat until pale cream in colour. Sift the flour and cornflour and fold into the egg yolk mixture.

In a saucepan, heat the milk to a simmer. Remove from the heat and pour slowly into the mixture, whisking all the time. Transfer the mixture to the pan and cook gently to thicken. If it starts to look a little lumpy, give it a whisk. Set aside to cool.

In a blender, blitz the raspberries and passion fruit pulp and seeds. Pass through a sieve into a large bowl. Add the cooled mixture and whisk together well.

To prepare the soufflé dishes, melt the butter and use to brush the inside each dish. Dust with icing sugar, shake to coat the sides of the dishes and tip out any excess.

In a clean, grease-free bowl, whisk the egg whites to form stiff peaks. Add one spoon of egg white to the fruit mixture and stir together briefly to loosen. Then, turning the bowl as you work, fold in the rest of the egg white until just incorporated.

Spoon the mixture into the prepared dishes, put on a baking tray and place in the middle of the oven.

Bake for 10–15 minutes, then turn down the oven to 150°C/300°F/Gas 2 until the soufflés have risen and feel just firm to the touch with a slight wobble underneath.

Dust with icing sugar and eat immediately.

CHERRIES
with RECIPES *by* GARY RHODES

Plump, juicy, ripe cherries picked straight from the tree are one of the joys of summer. Sweet, deep red, juicy flesh that will stain your fingers, but after enjoying such a rich culinary experience do we really care?!

In fact the history of the cherry tree in the UK goes back a long way beyond our childhood. The Romans first brought wild cherries into the UK and it is said you can trace old Roman roads by the lines of cherry trees growing alongside, self-seeded from the stones that the soldiers spat out as they marched. Cultivation started in 1533 when the UK's first cherry orchard was planted in Kent by King Henry VIII.

For hundreds of years, England enjoyed the home-grown crops of abundant cherry orchards. Varieties with wonderful, celebratory names like Frogmore Early, Napoleon and Waterloo. By the early twentieth century, the popularity of the cherry had reached a peak and it was Britain's favourite summer fruit. But in just the last 50 years, we've lost 90% of our cherry orchards and now import nearly all of the cherries we eat.

British cherry trees have a short fruiting season, about four weeks or so around June and July, depending on the weather. So the very best way to save our British cherries is to start buying and cooking with them when they are available. Use them to make sweet tarts or cooling sorbets. Or take inspiration from medieval kitchens and combine them with savoury meats, try succulent duck with vibrant cherry sauce. And to keep their flavour alive until the next season, bottle them in brandy or preserve as jars of cherry jam.

Look out for British cherries in season, ask which varieties they are or, even better, plant your own tree and enjoy the blossom of spring while anticipating a summer of delicious home-grown fruit.

WARM CHERRY SOUP

I first tried making a soup like this in my restaurant in Dubai. We shipped in British cherries especially, and I created this as an amuse-bouche. It went down a storm, so I have developed it further, and now I want you to enjoy making it at home. It fuses the wonderful flavour of the cherry with the hint of almond that you get from the stones. (Now I know you may have concerns that there is a minute amount of cyanide in the stones, but in this quantity, there is no danger to your health.) You might be surprised that a soup made with cherries can work, but I promise you it does. *Gary Rhodes*

Serves 6–8
900g cherries, stoned, half the stones reserved
200ml water
200ml red wine
50ml port
1 cinnamon stick
1 strip of lemon peel
2 tbsp caster sugar
2 tbsp cherry jam
salt and pepper, for seasoning
squeeze of lemon juice, for seasoning

Crush the reserved cherry stones and wrap them in a muslin bag. Put all the soup ingredients and the bag of cherry stones into a saucepan and bring to the boil. Simmer for 5–6 minutes. Remove from the heat and leave the cherries in the pan to infuse and cool until just warm. Remove the bag of cherry stones.

Place the cherries and the infusing liquid in a food processor and blitz to liquidize until smooth. Rest a fine sieve over a bowl and pass the soup through the sieve. Season with salt and pepper and a squeeze of lemon juice.

The soup is now ready to serve and is best eaten just warm with a swirl of sour cream on top, and a slice of toasted walnut bread on the side.

ROAST DUCK BREASTS
with CHERRY COMPOTE DRESSING

We've such an amazing heritage of growing cherries, yet we've allowed it to almost disappear. Cherries and roast duck are a classic match. Keeping the cherry flavour at its most vibrant, it complements beautifully the succulent meat it accompanies, the rich flavour and tenderness of the duck more than welcoming the fruity bite of the cherry compote dressing. *Gary Rhodes*

Serves 4

4 duck breasts
salt and pepper
16–20 baby turnips, scraped
  or washed
small knob of butter
225g baby spinach leaves
225g chanterelle mushrooms,
  trimmed and washed

Cherry compote dressing
knob of butter
1 red onion, finely chopped

juice of 1 orange
225g cherries, stoned
generous splash of Kirsch (optional)
100ml red wine
1 tbsp cherry jam
salt and pepper

Orange and herb butter
juice of 1–2 oranges
50g butter
salt and pepper
1 tsp of chives or tarragon, chopped

For the compote dressing, melt the butter in a saucepan and soften the onion over a medium heat until tender. Add the orange juice and allow to boil until almost dry. Add the cherries and flambé with the Kirsch, if using. Add the wine and jam and allow to reduce in volume to a syrup consistency. Season with salt and pepper and remove from the heat.

Using a sharp knife, score the skin in close lines across each duck breast. Season the duck breasts with salt and pepper and place skin-side down in a dry frying pan over a medium heat. Cook for 10 minutes, without turning, until a lot of fat is released and the skin has become golden brown and crispy. Turn the duck breasts over and continue to shallow fry for a few minutes until the meat is cooked medium-rare to medium. Remove the duck breasts from the pan and allow to rest. Put the pan and duck fat to one side.

Meanwhile, boil the turnips in salted water until tender, before draining and tossing in a knob of butter. Season with salt and pepper. Add the spinach leaves to the turnips, allowing the leaves to wilt. Fry the chanterelles in a little of the duck fat left in the pan for just a minute or two, before seasoning.

To make the orange and herb butter, put the orange juice in a small pan and boil until reduced in volume by two-thirds. Whisk in the butter and season with salt and pepper. Finally stir in the chopped chives or tarragon and remove from the heat.

Carve the duck breasts and arrange on plates, spooning the vegetables around the duck slices in a rustic fashion. Spoon over the compote dressing and finish with orange and herb butter.

CHERRY CLAFOUTIS
with VANILLA WHIPPED CREAM

I want everyone to fall back in love with the British cherry. And this dish helps show off our cherries at their very best, classic cherry clafoutis. It isn't difficult to make, it looks stunning on the table on a warm summer's evening and rounds off al fresco eating perfectly. But I urge you to wait for the season when our glorious cherries are ripe in June and July, serving the clafoutis just warm so it can show off its 'ripeness' too. *Gary Rhodes*

Serves 4

Clafoutis
2 large free range eggs
75g caster sugar, plus extra for dusting
40g plain flour
100ml double cream or crème fraîche
100ml milk
butter, for greasing
225g cherries, stoned

Vanilla whipped cream
150ml double cream
25g icing or caster sugar
1 vanilla pod, seeds scraped out

Preheat the oven to 180°C/350°F/Gas 4. Put the eggs and sugar in a large bowl and whisk together. Sift over the flour and whisk in well before stirring in the cream or crème fraîche and milk. Leave to rest for 10 minutes.

Lightly butter a large baking dish and sprinkle with sugar to coat. Scatter the cherries in the dish and gently pour over the batter.

Bake for 20–25 minutes until the batter is just firm to the touch. If it is too soft in the centre, bake for a further 5 minutes. Remove from the oven and allow to cool slightly before serving.

While the clafoutis is cooling, whip together the cream, sugar and vanilla seeds to soft peaks.

Serve with the vanilla cream spooned over the top.

CHERRY *and* ROSE SORBET

Serves 4
200g caster sugar
100ml water
300g cherries, stoned
juice of ½ lemon
1 tsp rose water

Put the sugar and water into a saucepan and slowly bring to the boil. Boil until all the sugar has dissolved and the liquid has become very thick and syrupy.

In a blender, blitz the cherries to a purée with a little lemon juice. Add the sugar syrup and rose water and taste. It should be quite sweet. Add more lemon or sugar as necessary.

Pour into an ice cream machine or a shallow container and freeze. (If you are not using an ice cream machine, don't forget to stir every 10 minutes until frozen, to break up the ice crystals.)

This will keep happily for up to a week in the freezer but is best eaten fresh.

It is wonderfully refreshing served on its own or with cake or a tart instead of cream.

CHERRY TARTS

Makes 6

Pastry

140g plain flour, plus extra for dusting
pinch of salt
70g unsalted butter, very cold and
   cut into small pieces
30g icing sugar
2 free range egg yolks
flour, for dusting

Filling

150ml double cream
1 free range egg
50g caster sugar
300g cherries, halved and stoned

You will need six individual 10cm tart tins.

Sift the flour into a bowl with the salt. Add the butter and rub together with your fingertips until the mixture resembles rough breadcrumbs (or pulse in a food processor). Sift in the sugar and mix briefly. Finally add the egg yolks and stir in with a spoon. Bring together to form a firm dough. When the dough just holds together, wrap it in clingfilm and refrigerate to rest for at least 30 minutes.

Preheat the oven to 150°C/300°F/Gas 2. On a floured surface, roll out the pastry and cut out circles to line the individual tart tins. Press the pastry firmly into the tins and rest in the fridge for another 15 minutes.

Bake the pastry cases for about 15 minutes, to firm up the dough before adding the filling.

Turn up the oven to 200°C/400°F/Gas 6. In a bowl, whisk the cream, egg and sugar. When the pastry has cooled slightly, fill the bottom of each case with cherries and pour in the cream mixture to fill.

Bake for about 25 minutes, the filling should be brown and slightly puffed up and the cherries soft.

CHERRY BRANDY

Makes   1kg cherries, stalks removed
1 litre   800g sugar
             1 litre brandy

You will need a 500ml jar for the first maceration and two 500ml glass bottles for the finished brandy.

Take the stones out of half of the cherries and crack the stones to bruise the kernels. Prick the other half of the cherries with a skewer. Mix all the cherries and cracked stones with the sugar and leave for about 30 minutes.

Put the sugared cherries into a sterilised jar and pour over the brandy to cover. Replace the lid and store in a cool, dry place to macerate for at least one month.

Strain through a muslin sieve, pour into sterilised bottles and seal immediately.

CABBAGE
with RECIPES *by* JASON ATHERTON

Cabbage has earned a poor and undeserved reputation which we are about to change. Let's celebrate this vegetable for being the tasty, versatile and nutritious crop that it is. Perfectly suited to UK cultivation and used in many of the worldwide cuisines we have embraced – Chinese, Italian and French among them. It's time to bring cabbage back home.

Be versatile with how you cook it. Crunchy and raw in salads, in a Northern Indian style curry, or as an autumnal dish cooked with chestnuts and bacon to accompany roast game. Whatever the season, cabbage has a worthy place in our cooking. Leafy, compact, pointy, frilly, the cabbage is a handsome and varied vegetable. It is also low in calories, rich in vitamins and minerals and a wonderful source of antioxidant vitamin C. It's good for eyes and skin, boosts immunity and cleanses the body – cabbage is a superfood! And yet, cabbage sales have fallen by 71% over the past 30 years and now farmers are forced to feed unsold crops to cattle.

There's a cabbage variety for every British season, so we don't need to rely on cabbage imports. Try different varieties and colours from white to emerald green to red. And don't just think of cabbage as a winter vegetable. The Hispi, a hearted or sweetheart cabbage as it is sometimes known, is a great summer vegetable. The leaves are more open than those of a winter cabbage and they have a softer texture and sweeter taste.

So all year round, eat cabbage raw or cooked in endless different ways, but most of all learn to love this vegetable for the flavour and texture it has to offer.

WHITE CABBAGE ESCABECHE
with FREE RANGE QUAIL *and* CHANTERELLES

I love to use white cabbage as the challenge is to do something a little different – as people always use this particular cabbage for coleslaw or pickle. So I have elaborated on this theme by turning it into a cabbage escabeche which is a traditional Spanish dish for preserving. I am heavily influenced by Spain and its natural cuisine. I have served this dish with quail and when using quail I always buy large birds and free range where possible. *Jason Atherton*

Serves 4–6

Escabeche salad
8 large white cabbage leaves
4 carrots, peeled and thinly sliced
4 shallots, broken down into petals
100ml white wine vinegar
100ml olive oil
3 garlic cloves
2 tbsp sugar
1 tbsp coriander seeds

Roasted quail
100g unsalted butter
50ml vegetable oil
salt and pepper
4 large quail
20 Scottish chanterelles
carrot tops, to garnish

Bring a large pan of salted water to the boil, add the cabbage leaves, carrots and shallots. Return to the boil and cook for 2 minutes. Drain and quickly refresh the vegetables in a large bowl of iced water. Drain, pat dry the vegetables and put in a heatproof dish.

Put the vinegar, oil, garlic, sugar and coriander seeds into a small saucepan, bring to boil, pour over the vegetables and leave to cool.

Preheat the oven to 180°C/350°F/Gas 4. Heat the butter and oil in a large frying pan. Season the quail with salt and seal in the frying pan, until brown all over, basting with the butter and oil as the meat browns. Place the quail on a roasting tray and put in the oven for 2 minutes. Using the same frying pan, cook the chanterelles for one minute. Season with salt and freshly ground black pepper.

To serve, place the quail on a plate with the chanterelles. Arrange the vegetables around the quail and drizzle over a little of the escabeche sauce. Garnish with carrot tops.

CABBAGE PESTO, STEAMED TURBOT *and* LINCOLNSHIRE POTATO ROYAL

Hispi cabbage is a great cabbage with which to do so many things. Braise it with chicken thighs, or simply cut in half and grill it with lemon and serve with fish in the summer. I have done this recipe to show you how easily you can adapt this vegetable. I have made a pesto with the leaves, to make a dressing for the king of fish, the turbot. I have also used the cabbage stems, again to demonstrate that no part of this should be thrown away. *Jason Atherton*

Serves 4
1 Hipsi cabbage
4 large portions of turbot
sea salt and pepper
30g pine nuts, toasted
30g Parmesan, grated
200ml olive oil
squeeze of lemon juice
500g Lincolnshire baby potatoes
500g Lincolnshire Poacher cheese, grated
1 tbsp crème fraîche
salt and pepper
50g chickweed

You will need buttered greaseproof paper.

Preheat the oven to 130°C/250°F/Gas ½. Separate the cabbage heart by removing the looser leaves from the outer layer but leaving the tighter centre leaves still attached to the stem. Bring a large pan of water to the boil, add the outer cabbage leaves and cook until tender. Remove with a slotted spoon into a bowl of iced water to refresh. Re-boil the water and put in the centre leaves. Cook until tender, then drain and quickly refresh in a large bowl of iced water.

Line a baking tray with the buttered greaseproof paper, season the turbot and place on the paper. Fold the paper over like a parcel and turn over so the fold is at the bottom. Put in the oven and cook for 7–8 minutes until just tender.

Put all the blanched cabbage leaves, pine nuts, Parmesan and oil in a blender and blend until smooth. Season with sea salt and lemon juice.

Meanwhile, cook the potatoes in a pan of boiling water. Drain and peel. In a small saucepan, melt the cheese with a little crème fraîche. Coat the potatoes in the cheese mix and season. Cut the blanched cabbage centre into quarters. In a pan, melt a little butter and fry until the cabbage starts to colour.

To serve, place the cabbage on a plate and top with a portion of turbot. Arrange the potatoes around the fish and cabbage, spoon over the cabbage pesto and garnish with chickweed.

RED WINE SPICED RED CABBAGE, PORK LOIN *and* CARAMELISED SHALLOTS

Red cabbage is my personal favourite and most cuisines seem to make use of this amazing cabbage. I love its adaptability; from the way you can pair it with game to serving it raw in salads. You can make a great autumnal purée for wild game-birds or mallard by cooking it down with red wine, port and apples, blend and then serve hot. I wanted to show in this recipe the amazing textures you can create with the king of cabbages. *Jason Atherton*

Serves 4–6	butter, for cooking	salt
	1 large red cabbage, sliced	vegetable oil
	1 head of garlic	
	750ml red wine	*Caramelised shallots*
	200ml port	butter, for cooking
	1 bouquet garni	8 banana shallots, peeled
	1 spiced bouquet (cinnamon	3 tbsp brown sugar
	bark, star anise, clove)	1 tbsp thyme leaves
	1kg free range pork tenderloin	100ml veal stock

Melt the butter in a large pan over a low heat. Add the cabbage and garlic and cover with a lid. Cook until the cabbage is soft and then add the wine, port and bouquets and simmer for about an hour until the cabbage is really soft.

Preheat the oven to 180°C/350°F/Gas 4. While the cabbage is cooking, cut the pork into equal-sized pieces and season with salt. Heat the vegetable oil in an ovenproof pan, put the meat into the pan and seal all over. Transfer to the oven and cook for 6 minutes.

Meanwhile, melt some butter in a frying pan and fry the shallots until they start to colour. Add the sugar and thyme and continue to fry until they are caramelised, then pour in the stock and cook until the shallots are tender and the stock has reduced to a sticky glaze.

When the meat has cooked, remove from the oven, cover with foil and leave to rest. Remove the cabbage from the heat, transfer to a food processor and blend to a smooth purée.

To serve, place the pork on a plate with a spoonful of the spiced cabbage purée, the shallots and some of the shallot glaze.

CABBAGE, RADISH *and* TAHINI SALAD

A delicious, crunchy, raw salad with a Middle Eastern-inspired dressing.

Serves 4–6
1 savoy cabbage, finely shredded
1 white cabbage, finely shredded
1 bunch of radishes, finely sliced
2 carrots, grated
mixed bunch of mint and parsley, leaves picked from the stem, finely chopped
2 tbsp tahini paste
1 tbsp water
juice of 1–2 lemons
3 tbsp olive oil
sea salt and pepper
1 tbsp black onion seeds (nigella)

In a large bowl, mix the cabbage, radishes, carrots and herbs.

In a small bowl, mix the tahini with the water and stir well to make a smooth paste. Add half of the lemon juice and mix well; the tahini will start to thicken with the addition of the lemon. Stir in the olive oil to loosen the paste to a sauce; the dressing should be the consistency of double cream. Season with salt and pepper and taste. It should taste quite lemony, so add more lemon juice if necessary.

Pour the dressing over the salad, season with more salt and pepper and sprinkle over the black onion seeds. Mix well and taste before serving.

Perfect to eat on its own, with other salads as a meze or as an accompaniment to grilled chops.

CABBAGE, POTATO *and* CHICKPEA CURRY

Serves 6

5 tbsp oil, for frying
2 onions, finely chopped
sea salt and pepper
4 garlic cloves, sliced
3 hot red chillies, deseeded and finely chopped
2½ tsp each cumin seeds and coriander seeds
1 tsp ground turmeric
½ tsp cayenne pepper
600g potatoes, cut into chunks
1 whole cabbage, weighing about 1kg, shredded
100ml water
4 tomatoes, skinned, deseeded and chopped
1 can of chickpeas, drained
coriander leaves, to finish
ground cumin, to finish

Heat the oil in a large saucepan with a lid, and gently cook the onion with a little salt until it is soft and sweet. Add the garlic and chilli and continue to cook for a couple of minutes.

Toast the cumin and coriander seeds by placing them in a dry frying pan over a medium heat until they start to crackle. Tip them into a pestle and mortar with the turmeric and cayenne. Grind to a powder and then add to the onions.

Add the potatoes and a little more salt and some pepper to the onions, and fry for a minute. Add the cabbage and 100ml water. Place the lid on the saucepan and cook gently, stirring occasionally until the potatoes are tender and the cabbage soft.

After about 15 minutes, add the tomatoes and chickpeas and cook everything together, with the lid off, for another 15 minutes for all the flavours to absorb.

Sprinkle with the coriander leaves and ground cumin and serve with yogurt and rice.

CABBAGE
with CHESTNUTS

Serves 4
as a side
dish

25g butter
50g smoked, streaky bacon, cubed
2 garlic cloves, finely sliced
250g cooked, peeled chestnuts, roughly chopped
1 large cabbage, shredded
200ml chicken stock
sea salt and black pepper

In a large saucepan with a lid, melt the butter and fry the bacon until it starts to crisp. Add the garlic and chestnuts and continue to cook for a minute or so. Add the cabbage and stir well. Fry everything together for about a minute until the cabbage begins to soften. Pour in the chicken stock and season with salt and pepper. Simmer gently, covered, for about 15 minutes or until the cabbage is completely soft.

Serve with roasted pork or game-birds.

SUPPLIERS

Here are the details for farms, growers, shops and other suppliers of the sixteen great British ingredients used in this book.

PEARS

Hayle Farm
Marle Place
Horsmonden
Tonbridge
Kent
TN12 8DZ
01892 732 807

JL Baxter & Sons
Amsbury Farm
East Street
Hunton
Maidstone
Kent
ME15 0QY
01622 820 844

HERBS

Jekka's Herb Farm
Rose Cottage
Shellards Lane
Alveston
Bristol
BS35 3SY
www.jekkasherbfarm.com
01454 418 878

Nicholson's Herb Farm
Willow Farm
Fenton Way
Chatteris
PE16 6UP
www.nicholsonsherbfarm.co.uk
01354 600 127

PLUMS

Fast Ferry Produce Ltd
Ascot Road
Pershore
Worcestershire
WR10 2JJ
www.ferryfast.yolasite.com
01386 552 131

Vale Landscape Heritage Trust
Field Barn, Evesham Road
Cleeve Prior
Evesham,
Worcestershire,
WR11 8JX
www.myweb.tiscali.co.uk/valetrust
01789 778 582

RHUBARB

E. Oldroyd & Sons Ltd
Hopefield Farm
The Shutts
Leadwell Lane
Rothwell, Leeds
West Yorkshire, LS26 0ST
www.yorkshirerhubarb.co.uk/
0113 282 8775

Simple Foods Kiosk
Clumber Park, Worksop
Nottinghamshire S80 3AZ
www.nationaltrust.org.uk/clumberpark/
01909 544 917

Thorpe Lane Farm
Thorpe Lane,
Thorpe
Wakefield
WF3 3BZ
01924 822 314

NUTS

JIB Cannon & Son
Roughway Farm
Roughway Lane,
Tonbridge
Kent, TN11 9SN
01732 810 260

Opies Pickled Walnuts
Chalkwell Road
Sittingbourne
Kent, ME10 2LE
www.b-opie.com
01795 476 154

Sharpham Park
Street, Somerset
BA16 9SA
www.sharphampark.com
01458 844 080

Walnut Tree Company
West Cottage
Flimwell
North Wadhurst
East Sussex
TN5 7PX
www.walnuttrees.co.uk
01892 890 376

BEETROOT

The Lost Gardens of Heligan
Pentewan, St.Austell
Cornwall, PL26 6EN
www.heligan.com
01726 845 100

Riverford Farm
Buckfastleigh
Devon, TQ11 0JU
www.riverford.co.uk
01803 762 059

COCKLES *and* MUSSELS

The Fish Society
Coopers Place
Wormley
Surrey
GU8 5TG
www.thefishsociety.co.uk
01428 687 768

The Seafood Company Wales
Swansea, Cardiff
SA4 8SG
01554 770 979

PEAS

The Balloon Tree
Farmshop and Cafe
Stamford Bridge Road
Gate Helmsley
York
YO41 1NB
01759 373 023

WR Haines
Castle Farm, Station Road
Chipping Campden
Gloucestershire, GL55 6JD
www.wrhaines.co.uk
01386 841 226

BEEF

Kingston Farm
Forfar, Angus
Scotland, DD8 2RU
www.dunlouiseangus.com
01307 462 784

Maydencroft Farm
Maydencroft Manor
Gosmore
Hitchin, Hertfordshire
SG4 7QA
www.maydencroftfarm.com
01642 420 851

Wimpole Estate
Arrington
Royston
Cambridgeshire
SG8 0BW
www.wimpole.org
01223 206 000

GARLIC

The Garlic Farm
Mersley Lane
Newchurch
Isle of Wight, PO36 0NR
www.thegarlicfarm.co.uk
01983 865 378

The Really Garlicky Company
'New Reekie'
Unit 14
Balmakeith Business Park
Nairn
Highlands of Scotland
IV12 5QR
www.reallygarlicky.co.uk
01667 452 193

TURKEY

Blackwells Farm Produce
Herons Farm
Colne Road
Coggeshall
Colchester
Essex
CO6 ITQ
www.blackwellsfarmproduce.co.uk
01376 562 500

Kelly Turkey Farms
Springate Farm
Bicknacre Road
Danbury
Essex
CM3 4EP
www.kellyturkeys.co.uk
01245 223 581

MACKEREL

The Cornish Fishmonger
Unit 4, Warren Road
Indian Queens Industrial Estate
Cornwall, TR9 6TL
www.thecornishfishmonger.co.uk
01726 862 489

Gavin Thain
Fraserburgh Harbour
Aberdeenshire
Scotland

Watercress Lane Farm
Mattishall
Dereham, NR20 3RJ
www.watercresslane.co.uk
01362 850 254

CURRANTS

Blackcurrants
Lower Lulham Farm
Madley, Hereford
HR2 9JJ
07976 761 773

Red and whitecurrants
Thomas Thomson
The Packhouse
Haugh Road
Blairgowrie
PH10 7BJ
www.tthomson.co.uk
01250 875 500

EGGS

Garden Quails
2 Churchlands Cottages
Kirdford, West Sussex
RH14 0LU
www.gardenquails.com
01403 820 796

Top Farm
Thursford Road
Great Snoring
Fakenham
Norfolk, NR21 0HW
www.topfarmeggs.co.uk
01328 820 351

CHERRIES

Lower Hope Farm
Ullingswick
Hereford
HR1 3JF
www.lowerhopefarms.co.uk
01432 820218

Park Farm Cherry Orchard
Lynstead
Sittingbourne
Kent, ME9 0JH
www.lynsted-orchard.org.uk
01795 520 256

CABBAGE

Marshall Brothers Farm
Mill Lane
Butterwick
Boston
Lincolnshire,PE22 0JQ
01205 760 461

New Farm Organics
New Farm
Soulby Lane
Wrangle, Boston
Lincolnshire
PE22 9BT
www.newfarmorganics.co.uk
01205 870 500

INDEX

ACKNOWLEDGEMENTS

Outline Productions, the company behind The Great British Food Revival would like to congratulate everyone who was involved in the television series for delivering such an engaging and enlightening show, and to those at Orion Publishing for creating such a beautiful and informative book. Special thanks must go to the all chefs and cooks whose co-operation and contribution to the project was invaluable. Their knowledge and passion for British heritage produce was infectious and the recipes they created featuring the endangered produce were absolutely mouth watering.

Particular thanks must also go to Lindsay Bradbury, the BBC Commissioning Editor, for all her advice and support. The entire production team of Marc Beers, Philippa Murphy, Alastair Bell, Sophie Seiden, Isaure de Pontbriand, Chris Vila, Victoria Balfour, Jessica Phillips, Alice Binks, David Warren, and Ellie Winstanley did an amazing job of finding and filming the stories on location. In the Food Revival kitchen, the director Emma Reynolds and her team covered the recipes so beautifully that they really did look too good to eat. Back at base, the hard work of Melany Hunt, Pollyanna Huntingford, Maisie Clater and Sean Schmolz did not go unnoticed and particular mention must go to Susie Staples, who as the producer of the series was the linchpin who held it all together.

The off-line editors of the series were Paul Clifton, Steve Flatt, Dan Raymond and Roy Williams and Full Broadside provided the on-line facilities. The graphics for the series were created by Patrick Brazier, Sharon Spencer and Sara Shabbar at The Station, the photography is courtesy of Andrew Hayes-Watkins and the music was composed by Dan McGrath and Josh Phillips. A very big thanks to you all.

At Orion, thanks to Amanda Harris and her team of Blanche Vaughan, Nicola Crossley, Sally Coleman, Natasha Webber, Kate Barr and Clare Hennessy for producing such a delicious book.

This book shines a light on those traditional British ingredients that may disappear forever if we don't do something about it. The best thing we can do is to start seeking them out and eating them again, and I hope the recipes in this book will inspire you to do so.

Bridget Boseley *Executive Producer, Outline Productions*